# BAYONNE BOY

*Bob Vargovcik*

authorHOUSE®

*AuthorHouse*™
*1663 Liberty Drive*
*Bloomington, IN 47403*
*www.authorhouse.com*
*Phone: 1-800-839-8640*

*Published by AuthorHouse  4/25/2012*

*ISBN: 978-1-4685-6231-6 (sc)*
*ISBN: 978-1-4685-6232-3 (e)*

# CHAPTER 1: EARLY CHILDHOOD

It all started on July 29, 1937. That's when I was born. Jersey City, New Jersey, was the place. I know what the title says, but I was born at Margaret Hague Maternity Hospital, which at that time was considered a pretty good hospital. Anyway, after a week, I arrived in Bayonne, where I would remain for the next forty-one years.

I loved Bayonne. It was a great place in which to grow up. It was a safe town, although back in those days most smaller towns were relatively safe places to raise children. The years 1936 through 1939 must have been prosperous. The country was just coming out of the Great Depression, and World War II wasn't a threat to us yet, so everyone decided it was safe to start raising a family. There were a bunch of us born in those years.

I grew up on East Twenty-Seventh Street, between Broadway and Avenue E: 25 East Twenty-Seventh, to be exact, right across the street from the Russian Club. It was all part of St. John's Church located on East Twenty-Sixth Street. That was the church that served the Russian community, and in my neighborhood and it was a big one. Half the block was Russian. And there was a bar located in the basement of the club, that served the men on the block. Mr. Drobovsky was the bartender. He lived right across the street from the club and two doors up from us. In fact, during World War II, he was our neighborhood air-raid warden.

To appreciate just how much the times have changed, try sending a six- or seven-year-old kid into a bar to buy a bucket of beer and two packs of Chesterfields. You will find yourself sporting a nice pair of orange coveralls and stainless steel bracelets. Yet, my mother would routinely hand me a buck, and off I would go to get the old man's provisions.

Bayonne is also where I met my wife, and for that alone the town will always be special. In fact, we actually met at The Venice Tavern down on Cottage Street. She was seventeen, and I was twenty-three. That was during July 1960. It took me two years to realize what was happening. We started dating in September 1962. We were partners in the wedding party of my friend Jim Slick, when he and his wife, Carol, were married. We have been together ever since.

My family lived on Twenty-Seventh Street until April 1949, when we moved to Humphreys Avenue. Most of the neighborhood kids were within one or two years of my age, so it was never boring. Back in the forties we owned the streets. There were very few cars on our block. For one thing, they did not produce any cars during World War II, and if you owned a car back then you had trouble getting tires or just buying gas, unless you were my father. We had tires on our car, even though they might have been of different sizes. And he always managed to get a tank of gas when we would make our pilgrimage to Union Beach, the poor man's Riviera.

When my sister and I were young, my father wheeled around in a 1933 Chevy four-door. It was black with red wire spoked wheels. But that all changed in 1942. When we were small my parents would often take us to spend weekends at my father's sister's house in Dunellen, NJ. Compared to

Bayonne, it was country living. We always looked forward to going there. The blue jays screeched all day, something we didn't hear in Bayonne, and we didn't smell the refineries. On one of our trips to Aunt Mary's house, we left in our '33 Chevy and came home in a huge 1936 Oldsmobile. My aunt Mary's landlord was having eye trouble and could no longer drive, so he made my father one of those legendary offers that you couldn't refuse, and he didn't. It had a straight eight-cylinder engine with two carburetors, a hood as long as a football field, and an interior to match. It was a beautiful automobile. The color was battleship gray, which in 1942 you could say was in style. It also had a trunk, something lacking in the Chevy. When we headed for Union Beach, we could load everything for one trip, including my cousin MaryJane.

Back then there were not a lot of women driving, but my mother was an exception. She was not daunted by the size of the Oldsmobile. She just got behind the wheel and off she went. It would be the last car my father would own. In 1952 he took it for a last spin, a one-way trip to Twin City Auto Wreckers. He came home on a Broadway bus with twenty-five dollars in his pocket and the car's radio under his arm. It was truly the end of an era.

The war started on December 7, 1941. I was four and a half years old. It ended in May 1945 against Germany and in September against Japan. I was eight years old. I remember those years. There was always something going on. The country was on a war footing, and patriotism was very much in vogue. Everyone from movie stars to garbage men did their part to win the war. I believe it was the last time this country was really united.

There was a naval base in Bayonne down at the old port terminal. It was booming during the war. It had a good-sized dry dock, plus plenty of docking space, which translated into lots of ships at dockside and lots of sailors up the street.

The main entrance to the base was at the foot of East 32 Street. About a ten-minute walk would get you up to Broadway, Bayonne's main street. That's where the spa and the two local watering holes were located, and it was where the sailors were separated from their money.

You could go up there any time of the day and see some kind of action, and it was only a five-block walk from where I lived. Now you ask, "How could a six- or seven-year-old kid roam that far from home on his own?" Well, back then there was very little traffic, and we didn't have the lunatics running around then. They seem to be coming out of the woodwork today. A kid was pretty safe on the street.

The Jersey Central Railroad ran right down the end of our street. The track ran to the Jersey City docks. We'd go down the street and be in awe of the trainloads of military hardware passing in revue—tanks, trucks, and planes, a lot of them coming out of the GM plant in Linden, NJ. Of course, Bayonne kicked in too. We had Esso, Gulf, and Tidewater Oil refining thousands of barrels of oil every day for the war effort.

At that time my father worked for Nelson Transportation as a captain on a small tug called the *C and C*. On Sunday afternoons my mother would pack up my sister and me, and we would go down to First Street and catch the ferry to Staten Island. Then we got the train to Mariner's Harbor. My father would be waiting at the dock with the *C and C*, and off we would go in our own little yacht. My father would take us out to the Narrows, where would see literally hundreds of ships waiting to form into convoys to make the dangerous Atlantic crossing to deliver their cargoes.

Sometimes my father would just cruise around the harbor, but most of the time the boat was working, so we would just go where the boat took us. I thoroughly enjoyed those afternoons, and I guess you could say that my future was sealed on those Sunday afternoons.

Of course wartime was not playtime. It was serious business. Men were fighting on all the different battlefronts, both the Atlantic and Pacific. Most of my uncles and even my cousin Billy were serving in the armed forces, and of course I was doing my part at home. I was now old enough and big enough to have my own ice wagon, and my father built me a beaut. It had a box big enough to carry a big payload; a long, heavy-duty tongue; and a set of hard-to-get solid rubber tires—a real mean machine. I put it right to work. I lugged flattened tin cans to the junkyard and collected cans of animal fat from the neighbors and took it to the butchers, but scrap paper was my main thing. I'd load my wagon up with bundles of old newspapers and haul it down to Library Court between Twenty-First and Twenty-Second Streets. I sold them for a penny a pound. After you delivered your first thousand pounds, you became a paper trooper, and for every hundred pounds after that you received a hash mark. I had my paper trooper patch sewn on my shoulder and hash marks running up my sleeve. My mother was thrilled. After a couple of weeks of humping newspapers, I received my lesson in capitalism and became a war profiteer in the process. I can talk about it now because the statute of limitations has run out on wetting the middle of a bundle of newspapers and covering it with dry paper.

As you probably know, we won the war. I very modestly accept my share of the credit, because it's a group effort. A good part of the credit has to go to the men in the trenches, the soldiers, sailors, and marines, and of course Mr. Drobovsky, our neighborhood bartender and air-raid warden, who would illuminate the front of your house with his flashlight to let you know that you had a sliver of light showing around your blackout shade.

If there ever were any enemy bombers overhead, we would definitely have been at ground zero.

I often wonder how educated people could worry about an air attack from a country located four thousand miles away. German bombers couldn't make the trip one way, let alone round-trip. But they were worried. The side of the streetlights facing the ocean were painted black to deter German U-boats. I couldn't figure that one out. If I couldn't see the Atlantic Ocean from the streetlight, how could the people on the U-boat see the streetlight from the ocean. Then my father had to paint the upper half of the car's headlights black so that—you got it!—those same bombers wouldn't catch us coming home from Grandma's house.

We never did get bombed, so I guess all those precautions we took were responsible for that. I'm sure those anti-aircraft gunners down at the oil refineries were just a little disappointed. I'm sure they wanted a crack at a German plane or two ,How could you tell your grandchildren that you spent the war in Bayonne, NJ, looking up at the sky for an enemy that never showed up? I know for a fact that Mr. Drobovsky wore his air-raid warden's helmet at many a Memorial Day parade. And he always received a round of applause as he passed Twenty-Seventh Street. For a job well done, not one bomb fell in our neighborhood.

# CHAPTER 2: ST. JOSEPH'S SCHOOL

All the time this war was going on, we had to get an education, and where else but St. Joseph's School. In order to attend, one of your parents had to be Slovak. It was a Slovak parish staffed by a Slovak priest and Slovak nuns. Sister Bertrand and Sister Pauline made sure that we could speak it and read it. The good nuns made sure that we learned. They had all the time in the world, and we were their mission in life. At St. Joe's, you paid attention, or else the yardstick was used for a lot more than pointing to the blackboard. And they had my mother's permission to use me for target practice.

In September 1942, I started kindergarten. I didn't like it. In fact, I kicked and screamed, and I almost kicked a door panel out. But like a rodeo horse, you eventually get broken, and they led me in like a zombie.

Kindergarten back then was not like it is today. Back then it wasn't mandatory, so the class was small. In fact, it consisted of one row in the first-grade class, the row by the windows. While the first graders were sweating over their assignments, we were chilling out with clay and construction paper.

And of course they didn't close school at the first sign of moisture, like they do today. Rain or shine, you showed up. Those who didn't were disdained as sugar babies. I lived two and a half blocks from school, so even though it was uphill both ways, I walked. Even if the snow was up to my butt my mother would bundle me up like an Eskimo and push me out the door. She reasoned that, if I stayed home from school, I would end up playing outside in the snow anyway.

When we finally got to school, there were one row of kindergarten kids and about twenty first graders to undress—snowsuits, scarves, mittens, and galoshes—plus those runny noses. By the time we were all undressed, it was lunchtime. After lunch it was time to start getting everybody dressed for the trip home.

While we were learning the three Rs, we were also reminded that there was a war going on. We had our air-raid and fire drills, and we learned how to put a fire out with sand and a hand-pumped fire extinguisher. We were each issued a fire proof ID tag, which we were required to wear at all times.

All in all, school wasn't that bad. I made a lot of new friends and expanded my horizons. I met Bill Nemik in kindergarten and Ron Koch in first grade. Life was good. I was getting good marks. That made my parents happy. I was also still in the tin can and scrap paper business, and that kept Uncle Sam happy.

In 1944, I was seven years old and in the second grade. It was time for me to make my first Holy Communion, a big step. The church told me I had reached the age of reason, and there were no more excuses. "You do wrong now, you own up." We learned about confession, contrition, and penance. Then it was off to church and the real thing. Thirty or so of us lined up outside the confessional ready to spill our guts. Confession is a private thing between you and the priest, but this day I thought the priest was in the rectory the way all these sins were echoing through the church. They were in that confessional telling the whole world how rotten they've been so far. This whole thing was done alphabetically. Since my last name started with V, I was way back in line. I was listening to all this and thinking, *My god! Where have I been? I've been too good. I've got to think up some winners or I'm going to look pretty lame when I get in there.*

Well, I pulled it off. I think the bit about cheating the government with the wet newspapers put me over the top. I heard some ooohing and ahhhing out there.

I received my first communion the following day. My mother had a party for me at the house. All of my aunts and those uncles who weren't with the military were there. I raked in a whopping fifty-one bucks. A lot of money in 1944.

The war ended in May 1945 over in Europe and officially in September in the Pacific. All of the men started to return home, and by 1946, things were pretty much returning to normal.

My father's 1936 Oldsmobile was still the only set of wheels on the Lee side of the family. My father's younger brother, Micky, had a 1941 Pontiac that he had put in storage. He was drafted into the navy in 1943 at the age of 36. He and my aunt Ronnie didn't have any children, so away he went. He served on aircraft carriers. He was aboard the USS *Sangamon* when she was hit by a kamikaze plane at Okinawa. She returned to the States for repairs, and he came home with her. In fact, I have a piece of that plane sitting on my desk.

# CHAPTER 3: THE VARGOVCIKS GO ON VACATION

Uncle Ziggy, my father's brother-in-law, had a 1938 Chevy. That car and my fathers' Olds was the extent of the family motor pool.

As far back as I can remember, we always went on a summer vacation. The Kennedys had Hyannis Port, and the Vargovciks had Union Beach, nestled on picturesque Raritan Bay, right between the cozy little hamlets of Keyport and Keansburg, NJ.

Up in Bayonne we would load up the trunk and backseat of the Olds until there was barely enough room for us to squeeze in. Off we'd go. My old man was a spender, while everyone else took Highway 25 to beat the tolls. We went through Staten Island and over the Bayonne Bridge, where he would ask for a combination ticket, which cost seventy-five cents. That got us over the Outerbridge Crossing for just a quarter. Once we passed the pirate ship on Route 36, we knew we were almost there. We always tried to arrive early in the day. These bungalows my parents rented usually took quite a bit of elbow grease to make them habitable. The first order of business was plugging the holes in the screens. Everyone was issued a roll of toilet paper and assigned a room. There were no windows as such, just screens and a shutter held up by a stick. In a gentle rain the shutters were enough to keep the rain out. If the wind blew, well, we closed the shutters and sat in the dark. We went into our assigned rooms and checked the screens for holes. Of course, sometimes we checked the holes for a screen. We would then roll up a wad of toilet paper and stuff it in the hole. Before we did the screen thing, my father went through the place, spraying with a flit gun. Hopefully, this drove the mosquitoes out of the place. The idea was to keep the critters out, not in.

None of these places had indoor plumbing. The outhouse was usually in the back and loaded with spiders. My father made short work of them with a torch. By supper time we were all moved in, ready to relax and enjoy all that Union Beach had to offer.

We always had a lot of company when we were at the shore. You could catch a train from Bayonne to Union Beach, with just one change at Elizabethport. Of course, as the family motor pool got bigger, it became a lot easier, just a one-hour drive to sun and fun.

One summer—it had to be in the early 1940s—we arrived at our summer retreat, unloaded the Oldsmobile, took care of the screens and the outhouse, went shopping for groceries and ice (no fridge), and went for a swim thanks to an afternoon high tide, the only time you could actually swim. At low tide you went for a wade. We returned to the bungalow and had supper. Then the old man hooked up the old Philco Cathedral radio, ran a wire out the window as an aerial antenna, listened to the news with Gabriel Heeter, and got the latest war updates. In the meantime I caught up on the latest episode of "Superman" and the latest coded message from Kellogg's Pep cereal for my secret decoder ring. I was also anxiously waiting for the arrival of my secret Nazi-catching spy ring, which allowed me to see behind me without turning around and let me shake off any German spies on my tail. Because of his superpowers, the man from Krypton could pack an awful lot of axis spy fighting into one half-hour episode. He flew to the West Coast to deal with some Japanese sub trying to sneak into San Francisco and then back to New York to deal with a group of German spies landing on Long Island from a U-boat. In thirty minutes we were all out of danger for another day, except on Friday. With the weekend we were safe for two days.

After a couple of games of put-n-take, my father made a couple of passes around the house with the flit can to send a message to any marauding mosquitoes in the area. Then it was off to bed with us after he put a bucket in the kitchen to save a night run to the outhouse.

The next morning dawned brightly, but with such a clatter that my sister jumped out of bed to see what was the matter. And before our sleepy eyes could unfold was none other than Uncle Artie, Aunt Dottie, and the Dugan household. My sister were simply elated, but my parents, I'm sure, were completely deflated. Uncle Art and Aunt Dot were a barrel of cheer. It would be my old man who would pay for the beer.

Uncle Artie was a character. Most of the time he couldn't rub two nickels together, but he got a lot of mileage out of the one nickel that he did have. He was married to my father's sister, and they had three little Dugans, Bob, Eileen, and Ken. They arrived in an old Hudson (vintage unknown). Riding with Uncle Artie could sometimes be a pleasant experience. He usually had the road to himself. His car could just about keep up with the traffic flow, so passing was out of the question, and it blew so much smoke out of the exhaust pipe that no one could ride behind him for very long. So he more or less had his own piece of highway all to himself.

Whenever we made the trip down to Murphy's Bar or to the A&P, we all piled into the Olds. It was a great week with the Dugans. Uncle Artie and my father put away gallons of beer and bushels of crabs and clams. Aunt Dottie and my mother cooked up some great meals. My sister and I, along with the Dugans, had a great time swimming, crabbing, and going over to Keansburg to go on the rides.

All good things must come to an end, so it was with us. My father had to get back to work so we could afford another vacation, and Uncle Artie had to go back to his job in Jersey City. We left first, my father preferring not to ride behind Uncle Artie's Hudson

Even when we weren't on vacation, visiting the Dugans was a gas. They lived in downtown Jersey City on the fourth floor of a cold-water flat. Whenever we were coming, Uncle Artie would keep a sharp eye out for the Olds. When we pulled up to the curb, he would lower the beer bucket for the old man to fill up at the corner saloon. Before he came upstairs, Uncle Artie was the model of efficiency when it came to beer distribution. Poor Uncle Artie didn't last very long. He was in his midthirties when he died, leaving Aunt Dottie with three kids to raise. Eileen came to live with us for a while and scared my sister half to death every night with her ghost stories.

After the war, my parents and grandparents on my mother's side took the plunge and bought a place. It was located on Bayview Avenue, the higher class neighborhood in Union Beach. It had indoor plumbing and came with a fourteen-foot boat. It wasn't much of a place. It was open underneath, just sitting on cinder blocks. The rooms were laid out like office partitions with no ceilings. One could just climb over the wall into the next room. The kitchen had a gas stove, circa 1914. The bathroom was not actually a bathroom. It had no bathtub, just a commode, but it still beat the hell out of the outhouse. At bath time we just dragged a galvanized washtub in there, filled it with water, and rubba dub dub. My father gradually fixed the place up. He closed in the bottom and installed a ceiling and a new stove.

We would spend the entire summer there. I had friends both in Bayonne and Union Beach. There was a creek down at the end of our street. At high tide the swimming was great, and so was the crabbing and eeling. At low tide the depth of the water dropped to about a foot. We couldn't swim, but we would go clamming. We went with Uncle Ziggy. We'd take a pitchfork and a bucket and walk along the creek bed. When we saw a piss clam piss up through the mud, we would dig him up with the pitchfork. When we filled the bucket, we took it home, steamed the clams, and had them for lunch. We called that living off the fat of the land.

We never really made much use of the boat, though. We didn't have a dock down the creek, and it was just too heavy to lug around. One thing it was used for was picture taking. All our visitors would sit on it to have their picture taken. We were a family of fanatical picture takers, and I think most of the pictures taken ended up with me. I have boxes full of them. Every so often I go through them. It's a real trip down memory lane.

We had to sell the place when my grandfather died. I was never sure of all the circumstances, but we ended up selling it. I really missed the place. As I said before, I had a few friends in Union Beach, and I wouldn't be seeing them anymore.

But life goes on. The war was over. Everyone had good-paying jobs and money to spend, but nowhere to spend it. One place to spend some of it was a season membership to Murray's Lake, a little man-made lake—or I should say pond—located up in North Jersey, I think around Kinnelon. During the war, my aunt Rita worked with Murray down at the navy base. When he opened the lake, we took a ride up there to have a look at the place. We liked what we saw, a nice little man-made lake. My wife would love it. There were no sharks or crabs to grab her. There were diving boards, sliding ponds, a little beach, and plenty of picnic tables under the trees. We were up bright and early Sunday mornings to go to early mass. There were no Saturday evening masses back then. And then we went back home to start loading up the cars for the trek up to the lake. Union Beach was slowing but surely fading further and further into family lore by this time.

Our grand old Olds was by now getting on in years. Though she was still part of the family, she was no longer the pride of the fleet,We now used her for the most part for errands around town, but that was it. My parents, my sister, and yours truly were now reduced to mooching rides. By this time there were quite a few cars in the family, so we always got a seat with someone.

Uncle Vince got his driver's license and then went out and purchased a 1947 Studebaker with overdrive. If you wanted to get the hell scared out of you, go for a ride with Uncle Vince. When in overdrive on the highway, the car's wheels would be turning faster than the engine, a great gas saver, except Uncle Vince would forget about it. He'd ride around town with the damn thing engaged. All his cornering was of the two-wheeled variety, a trip up to Murry's lake with Uncle Vince could be exilerating,

On the way home from church on Sunday morning, my uncle Andy would swing by Davis's Icehouse, and we would load up with ice for the coolers, which were nothing more than galvanized washtubs covered with canvas. But they did the trick, and the ice usually lasted all day. Meanwhile, back at the house, the women would have the food and drinks ready to go. When the ice arrived, all the food was loaded, and off we went for a day of fun in the sun. But first we had to fight about three hours of traffic. Back in the late forties and early fifties, Route 17 consisted of only two lanes, one north and one south. We would make great time until we got to Paramus. That's where Route 4 from the George Washington Bridge joined Route17, and we came to a screeching halt. That's where I learned a lot of great words, expressions, and hand gestures that would serve me well through my adult life, especially when I drove a truck in New York City.

The weekly trips up to the lake continued for a few more years. Then we just stopped going. I wasn't too upset over it. When you reach the early teens, that family outing thing seems kind of tame and little embarrassing. I guess I was about fourteen when I started hanging out down at Billy Vandobec's barge, it was located down at the foot of East Thirtieth <u>Street</u>.

# CHAPTER 4: TEEN YEARS

In the <u>morning</u> I'd cross Avenue E and the railroad tracks and wait for the Lehigh Valley Railroad switch engine to go by. He would have a string of about fifteen cars going to the Hook. I would grab on and get a ride down to the barge. They frown on that sort of thing today, but back then there was someone hanging on every car. That train was more dependable than the bus,and cheaper,. I got home in the evening the same way. We had a great time at the bay. We spent our time crabbing, swimming, and fishing—or more precisely, eeling. They were about the only type of fish we caught. No other fish could survive. Crabs abounded. You could fill a bushel basket in fifteen minutes. And they were all big and full. Three or four of them made lunch.

With a couple rowboats at our disposal, our horizons were widened. We'd put Ronnie Koch's seven-and-a-half– horse, Elgin Outboard Motor, on one of the boats, and off we'd go. trolling for striped bass At Robbin's Reef Lighthouse. Life was good.

One of our escapades almost turned into a disaster. We found this old rowboat down at what we called the million-dollar pier. There was no million dollars and no pier. Everyone called it that, and I don't know why. Just one of life's little mysteries. Anyway, we decided to run the boat around to the Long Docks, which were located at the foot of East Forty-Ninth Street. Now the bay is at East Thirtieth Street. And the Long Docks were separated by the navy base. That was at the foot of East Thirty-Second Street. Everything was at the foot of something in Bayonne.

It was a cold April morning when we set sail from the millions. It was overcast and blustery. The crew consisted of Bill Nemik, Ron Koch, John Stoff, and myself. I was made captain because my father worked on a boat. We were sailing right along, enjoying the sights and the sea air until we were off the end of the navy base, actually about halfway there—the point of no return. The sea started picking up, along with commercial traffic (i.e., big tugboats and barges). We were dwarfed by these Leviathans. What really upset us, though, was the fact that our little rowboat was literally coming apart at the seams. Water was pouring in fore and aft port and starboard. Luckily we had the foresight to bring plenty of pumps. We each had a Maxwell House coffee can. We were scooping like hell with one hand, holding the boat together with the other hand. I don't know who was steering, but we made it safely to the Long Docks. To add insult to injury, the guy who owned the boat found out where it was and came and got it, the wreck that it was. That ended our short-lived plunge into piracy and our chance to breathe the rarified air surrounding boat owners.

## Teen years

At any rate, life as we knew it up to now was about to change. Girls entered the picture. Scavenging junk from abandoned barges no longer sounded like a cool way to make a buck. One needed a more dignified way to make money. I tried my hand at delivering Western Union telegrams. The job paid minimum wage—at that time sixty-five cents per hour plus tips. Happy telegram, good tip; sad telegram, no tip. So your pay could be fairly good, depending on your telegram. Actually, the downside of the job was the weather. Rain or snow, out you go.

About that time Bill Nemik got a job at a place called Foodserver located on Fourteenth Street and Avenue E. It was a cut-rate food market run by two brothers, Mortie and Eddie Siegler. Bill talked me into quitting Western Union and coming to work with him. Again, the minimum wage was sixty-five cents per hour. My first assignment was eyeing old potatoes. The Siegler brothers would buy potatoes so old they looked like an octopus. My job was to make them look presentable and, of course, sellable. The downside of the job was that, after eyeing one or two hundred pounds of potatoes, your hands were embedded with mud. No amount of scrubbing would get them clean. If anyone questioned my not-so-clean hands, I told them I was a mechanic. Back then, a mechanic was somebody.

And then we discovered Murdoch's Candy Store. It was located at Forty-Fourth Street and Broadway, just up the street from where I lived. I caught the bus for high school at that same corner. And it was also where I met a fellow by the name of Jim "Beak" Slick. He lived right up the street on West Forty-Fourth. He introduced me to the gang hanging out there. Pretty soon Bill Nemik and John Stofic came around, and for the next four years it became the place to hang.

This was 1952. We were all about fifteen years old, too young to drive. But there were a couple older guys with cars, so mobility was not a problem. Cruising Broadway became the thing to do: radio blaring, blowing the horn at every second car going in the opposite direction, and checking out the girls. Of course, the radios were all tuned to the station playing that new rage in music known as rock 'n' roll and a song called Blue Moon of Kentucky, by some yokel named Elvis Presley, another wannabe.

At age fifteen I started smoking. Bill Nemik got me started with some Viceroys he swiped from his mother. We couldn't afford a pack of cigarettes, so we bought Loosies four butts for a nickel. The brand will forever be printed in my mind: Wings. They tasted not unlike a piece of rope. Bill Nem and I hung around together quite a bit. We both had strict parents and stricter curfews. The witching hour was 10:00 PM. No excuses. It was in the door on the dot of ten or else. Mr. Emming was a neighbor who lived two houses up on Forty-Third Street. After I had joined the army, I came home on leave and met him in front of his house. He told me how much he missed me and how he used me to check his clocks. If they said it was ten o'clock, he would step out on his porch. If he saw me hauling ass down the street, he knew they were right on the money. Lights-out in the barracks was 2200 hours, or ten o'clock. I was well trained for that aspect of army life.

Anyway, Bill and I didn't have wheels, so if we didn't jump into somebody's car, we walked. Sometimes we would set pins at Yank n' Andy's or the Central Y Bowling Alley, and sometimes I would end up holding his coat and acting as his second while he duked it out with somebody. There was never a dull moment.

After my career change from Western Union to Foodserver, we ended up working together. We also recruited Jimmy Slick. He was now chief potato eye remover , and I moved up to produce trimmer. I also bagged and priced— heady stuff for a fifteen year -old.

For some reason there were a lot of cute girls shopping in the store. Boobs were in, and we had our own rating system, much to our boss's chagrin. We would check them out as they came in. There were the cupcakes with raisins and the coffee cakes with prunes. If I was at one end of the store and he was at the other end, I would yell, "Hey, Bill, check out coffee rings with prunes coming in! Or it might only be a cupcake with raisins. No big deal. Then, of course, Arlene from across the street would come in. We had a thing going. We'd disappear behind the sugar bags for a while. And Mortie, our boss, would be a wreck. Foodserver was a fun place. We once pulled an old lady out of the frozen food case. Everybody knows the fresh stuff is on the bottom, and she was going to get it. A customer came to the front and said there was a woman in the frozen food case. Sure enough, there she was upside down, with those ugly rolled-up stockings that old ladies wore. We pulled her out. She was holding on to that fresh box of frozen whatever, and she was happy. Mission accomplished.

While all this was going on, I was still primarily a student—and at this point not as good a student as I could be. My first four periods were in shop, working on engines, which I liked. The other stuff—algebra, civics, and whatever—left a lot to be desired. And it showed on my report cards. I was getting a little flack at home.

To the rescue came Mr. Manfreda our guidance counselor. It seems he had a friend in need of a helping hand. He owned a summer camp that was ravaged by a hurricane, and he was in need of extensive repairs in order to open for the coming summer season. We were recruited for the job. It was the spring of 1953, and we were driven out to Easthampton, Long Island, where the camp was located. Back then Easthampton was not the big-bucks area that it is today. It was mostly potato farms.

We would arrive Friday evening, have a fantastic dinner cooked up for us by a woman named Jessie, hit the sack early, get up bright and early, and eat a huge breakfast of eggs, bacon, sausage, and pancakes with lots of butter and maple syrup. They hadn't invented cholesterol yet. Then we'd go out and bust our asses, but it was good work. The air was fresh and salty. There was no pollution here. We built bulkheads and corrals, repaired roofs, got their fire engine and tractor running, and more or less overhauled the place and got it in shape for the summer season. We must have done a good job. We were rehired for the following year. And amazingly my marks improved. Politics, I presume.

While working at Camp St. Regis, I put in the hardest days' work of my life, and that includes up to the present time. The camp owner purchased about a mile of abandoned right of way from the Long Island Railroad. It ran somewhere between Riverhead and Montauk, and it was out in the middle of nowhere . It seemed he wanted the railroad ties for bulkhead material.

Bright and early one fine morning, after devouring one of Jessie's humongous breakfasts, off we went—not unlike lambs to the slaughterhouse. We rode out on two 1939 Ford flatbeds, which in happier days were used to cart potatoes in from the fields. When we arrived at the scene of the crime, we were relieved to see that someone had already removed the rails. In our eagerness to finish the job, no one noticed the terrain. The track ran through a cut with an embankment about ten feet high on either side of the tracks, made up of cinders.

We jumped off the trucks, anxious to get this over with. We were using tie tongs, which resemble ice tongs, except they have a wooden handle at the top. And they're carried by two men. We had four men to a tie, two in front and two in back. We'd pick up a tie—which wasn't light, even for four of us—and start up the embankment, and there we were marking time. The cinders didn't provide any traction. It was like walking on a treadmill, except that we had a hundred pounds of railroad tie between us.

It took us all morning and part of the afternoon to load the two trucks. End of story. No way! On the ride back, we figured we had it licked. We did the hard part. Unloading would be a breeze. Bang! We jumped down, and sure enough, one tire disintegrated and the inside tire was right behind it. We quickly unloaded the truck before the other tire blew! Luckily we had a spare. We'd change the tire and still make it back early. Nope. We put the jack under the truck and started jacking. No luck. Too much weight. We had to unload the whole damn truck, change the tire, and reload it again. By now it was dark, but we were all loaded up and ready to roll. We'd just take it easy going back. But we had no headlights. These trucks never ran at night. They brought potatoes in from the fields. That was done in daylight hours. Who checked headlights?

It was a dark night, and the tires didn't need a couple hundred pounds of live wood riding on top of all that dead wood. So we ended up walking in front of the trucks, pointing out the road so that they wouldn't end up in a ditch. It happened a long time ago, but I remember it as if it were yesterday.

# CHAPTER 5:

After we sold the place in Union Beach, Bayonne was the only show in town, except for the Sunday trip to Murray's Lake. Summers were spent either at Bill Vandobec's barge down the bay at East Thirtieth Street or in the Twenty-Seventh Street neighborhood. Playing ball was the big thing on Twenty-Seventh Street. If we weren't playing baseball in the Lincoln School yard on Twenty-Sixth Street, we were playing stickball or diamond ball in the street. You hardly ever see those games being played anymore. In fact, you never see them being played. But they were great low-budget games. All you needed for a game of diamond ball was a pink Spaldeen and a good-size piece of chalk, plus about sixty feet of clear curb space on each side of the street. And therein lay the problem. I don't think you can buy that much curb space today, with people fighting over parking spaces. Ditto with stickball.

Here are the rules for diamond ball. There are a minimum of four players on each team. Otherwise, in a bases-loaded situation, we would all be looking at each other with no batter. We used a good-size piece of chalk to mark the lines from first to second and third to home. The curb took care of home to first and second to third. You then made a diamond about eight inches across and about two feet long in front of the batter's box, and you chalked it up really well. The ball was pitched on one bounce, and the batter hit it with an open palm. The ball had to hit the ground between the baselines or he was out. Hopefully the ball would be fielded à la baseball and he would be out. If the pitched ball bounced in the chalked diamond, the batter had to swing or he was out. That was the reason for the chalk. It saved a lot of arguing. The ball was not that easy to hit. A good pitcher would use a lot of English on the ball, and it would be a son of a gun to hit.

There were a couple different variations of stickball. When I was a kid on Twenty-Seventh Street, there were only two cars on the whole street, and my father owned one of them. There was plenty of room for a game. Manhole covers were home and second. Curb sewers were first and third. You needed a pink Spaldeen and broom handle. If we had neither, it didn't matter. We would just check out the sewers,. Someone was always losing a ball there,. We would then open the sewer cover and lower some intrepid soul down, and he would grab the ball between his sneakers and we'd hoist him out with half of our equipment. The next thing we needed was a bat. For that we would scout the back porches until we spotted somebody's broom. We would borrow it, saw off the handle, and we were in business. The game was played like baseball when we played in the street, except that all putouts were made at home plate. Another variation was played against a wall, preferably between two buildings about a hundred feet apart. On one wall you drew a square about two feet wide and three feet high and chalk it up really well, again to prevent arguments. That would be the strike zone. Then you marked off imaginary lines on the other building, which would be your doubles, triples, and homers. Two could play. Simple, isn't it? Also, we can't forget box ball, which was played on the sidewalks up Broadway which were laid out in big squares it took four squares, one man to a square, and we smacked a ball at each other, trying to score points in a poor man's game of tennis.

Naturally in the autumn—after the World Series, of course—all thoughts turned to football. We played a variation called association. Footballs were expensive. We weren't talking a twenty-nine–cent Spaldeen or a nickel Rocket baseball here. Footballs were big bucks. When we did get a real football to kick around, it usually had a wad of tape plastered on each end to keep the bladder from popping out through the leather cover. What we usually tossed around was yesterday's newspaper, all rolled up into a tight cylinder and wrapped with a roll of masking tape. You couldn't kick it, but you could throw a mean bullet pass. The *New York Daily News* made the best—I guess I would have to call it a missile. It would be quite a stretch to call it a football. In a pinch, the *Bayonne Times* or the *Jersey Journal* would do. The game was played with four to eight players. Two opposing players would face each other, one with the newspaper. The rest of the players would run downfield to either catch a pass or defend against one. The man with the ball could elect to either run with the ball or pass to an open man. It was a great street game. Of course, with enough players and an empty lot, we would play the real thing, or a reasonable facsimile. Because of the lack of any protective equipment, tackling eventually led to a lot of—not exactly life-threatening injuries, but game-threatening injuries. A lot of players were being kept in by worried moms who thought the game was too dangerous. So we switched to two-hand tackle. There was no blocking, and laying two hands on the ball carrier at once was considered a tackle.

By far the biggest events of the summer were the boat rides, The Democrats and the Republicans each ran an excursion boat that left the city dock down on First Street and cruised up the East river into long Island Sound, finally docking at Rye Beach N.Y where we spent all of our money in the amusement park ,and eating junk food.

The boat usually arrived back in Bayonne in the late evening we all left the boat tired happy and broke. We usually ended up walking home for the lack of bus fare.

There was another boat ride sponsored by the Police Athletic League. This ride took us to Rockaway beach, in Brooklyn On the 1955 boat ride I met Joan Szyn. She was a cute little blonde and a twirler in the PAL band. I was determined to spend the day with her. She had something on the side of her nose, and I figured that was my opening. "Excuse me," I said, "you have something on the side of your nose."

She just looked at me. "That's a birthmark, stupid."

"Okay," I replied, "you know my name. What's yours?" I felt like an idiot, but she just laughed.

She said Joan,  what's your real name?" We spent the rest of the day together and had a great time.

I saw her a few times after that when I came home on passes or leaves from the Army. When I was discharged, I never called her I don't know why,. I fell in with bad company, and they introduced me to the Venice,a bar located on Cottage Street in downtown Bayonne That's where I met Barbara.

It was in January 1959. We went out for three and a half years, during which time her mother drove me crazy. I would arrive to pick her up for a date, and her mother would inform me that Barbara could not go out that night. She didn't finish her chores. This was a twenty-one-year-old girl we're talking about here. The final straw was my twenty-fifth birthday in 1962. We were at a friend's house, having a little party, when who storms in uninvited but none other than Mama, dragging Barbara out. She didn't finish her ironing. That was my last date with Barbara.

# CHAPTER 6:

In April 1949, we moved lock stock and barrel to 157 Humphries Avenue. It was situated between west Sixth and West Seventh Streets. We rented, of course. The house was owned by Mr. And Mrs. Stabler. He was a Bayonne cop, and she and Mrs. Yurik from Twenty-Seventh Street were sisters. That's how we got the place. Our landlord on Twenty-Seventh gave the house to his son and moved to an apartment. The son wanted the rooms for his in-laws, so out we went to a better neighborhood. Humphries was nice. We traded in the coal stove in the kitchen for a kerosene stove. Now instead of lugging a bucket of coal up to the kitchen every morning, I lugged a five-gallon tank of kerosene up two flights to boot. We still had the coal furnace in the cellar to heat the rest of the house, but it was a hot-air job and you woke up in the morning with a nose full of soot.

It was shortly after we had moved that I had a really bad day. It was in June 1949. I was up in the Sullivans' yard. In fact, I was up in a tree in their yard. It was on the corner of Fifth and Humphries, right up the street. I decided it would be easier to jump down from the tree than climb down. Bad decision. When I jumped, I hit a small branch sticking out. It snapped off and was driven up into the left side of my butt. I hit the ground, minus the left leg of my pants, and I saw these little round things that looked like BBs coming out of my leg. I started limping home. When some good Samaritan put me in his car and drove me home, I ruined his car seat. By now I was bleeding pretty badly. I dragged myself up the back stairs and into the bathroom, where I commenced to bleed all over the floor. I was so quiet that I probably would have bled to death if my mother hadn't looked in to see what was going on. She let out a scream, and in came my father. I figured I was pretty bad when he didn't holler at me. Instead he scooped me up and carried me down to the Oldsmobile. Instead of going to Grandma's house, we all went to the emergency room at Bayonne Hospital. And that was where my problems started. The ER doctor decided to sew me up. He then sent me up to the ward to spend the night. The next morning, Dr. Maderas, who was my grandma Lee's family doctor, looked at me and decided the gash was too deep and should heal from the inside out, so he removed the stitches. I spent five days in the hospital and was sent home cured—or so they thought. I wasn't done yet. This happened in June the following November. I started having problems. My left thigh started to turn black and swollen. They put me in the hospital, checked me out, and took X-rays but couldn't find anything.

I came home from the hospital but had to go to the doctor's office every week to get my leg drained. What a drag that was. Finally, the good doctor told my mother that if they couldn't check the blood poisoning, they would have to amputate. But in my case it would amount to cutting me in half. That wouldn't do. With nothing to lose, they decided to open me up. In December, just before Christmas, they operated and gave me—and I'm sure my mother—a great Christmas present. From way up in my left butt cheek, they pulled this mass out. It was a piece of the branch all wrapped up in tissue the size of an Alka-Seltzer jar, which is where it has been to this day—in an Alka-Seltzer jar on my end table drawer. This is a reminder of how stupid and lucky we can be sometimes. I've worn a scar on the back of my thigh as a constant reminder.

In 1951, I graduated from St. Joesph's School, and—much to the chagrin of a lot of people, including my principal, Sister Edwardina, and my mother—I opted to go to General Pulaski Technical And Vocational High School. I had hopes for the Merchant Marine Academy, but my eyesight wasn't good enough, so I settled. I took a course in power engineering. It dealt with propulsion systems ,gas, diesel,and steam, turbine and reciprocating. I enjoyed Tech, as it was called. I found the course interesting, and the rest of the classes were a gas. There was gym with Mike Stengler, which consisted of forty-five minutes of dismounted drills—hut 2, 3, 4, left flank, right flank to the rear march, etc. When I joined the army, I was way ahead of everyone else. Then there was Miss Bailoff. She taught us ancient history, a subject about as interesting as watching grass grow, but she livened it up by constantly reaching in and adjusting her bra straps and giving a bunch of fourteen-year-old boys a sneak preview of coming attractions.

Miss Buckmeyer taught us science. Her classes were enjoyable. She was not only a good teacher, but she also had the biggest set of boobs among the female faculty.

Miss Morganstern taught us civics. The class loved to watch her write on the blackboard. Her butt wriggled at the same speed as her writing.

Mr. Singer taught us English. He must have contracted

malaria or some exotic disease during the war. He would doze off in midsentence and leave us staring at the blackboard until the bell rang.

Mr. Brady taught us drafting. He had a glass eye. Enough said.

Mr. Berman ran the school. He was the principal. He was considered by many to be an expert in vocational education. He was respected by all the students. His big thing was smoking, or rather catching you smoking in the boys' bathroom. He would have the unlucky ones line up in the office and wait for their parents to come and bail them out.

I breezed through high school and graduated in June 1955. What would I do now? All my friends were joining the military, but I was not ready yet. I still had my eye on the merchant marine. But it was a bad time. Larger ships were being built to replace older, smaller ones, and that meant there was a surplus of seamen. I was stuck in a dead-end job on the shipping dock at the Maidenform Brassiere Company. Drastic measures were called for. I enlisted in the U.S. Army. On December 6, 1955, I marched off on my great adventure, or rather I was driven off. I was picked up at my house by a staff sergeant driving a 1952 Chevrolet and driven to the military induction center in Newark, NJ. There I was, sworn in and received my first command. They gave me a stack of paperwork for four other recruits and five train tickets. I was then ordered to report to the reception center at Fort Dix, NJ., pretty heady stuff for a scared recruit. It wasn't as bad as I thought it would be. When the train pulled into the station in Trenton, NJ, much to my relief there sat a Chevy Suburban driven by another staff sergeant. I didn't know where the hell Fort Dix was, let alone where to find the reception center. Anyway, I was off and running. Pvt.

E.1 Robert J. Vargovcik RA 11323447, A serial number that you never forget. I don't think there is anyone who ever served in the military who could not rattle off that number without a second's hesitation.

# Chapter 7: Welcome to the U.S. Army

The reception center was a place that you wanted to get over with and get behind you. This is where the army starts to cut you down to size. The first thing to go is your hair. We were all marched to the barbershop. We had a big laugh when asked, "How would you like it cut, young man?" Some of the more naive recruits actually told the barber—and I use that word loosely—how they would like their hair cut. He then shaved them clean.

Uniforms were next. We were marched to another building. We went in one door. There we were measured up—waist, inseam, neck, arm length, hat size, etc. Shoes and boots were another matter great care was taken when they measured for shoe size. We were going to do a lot of marching. This was the infantry.

After all the measuring was over, we all lined up in front of this counter, and as they called your name, you stepped up to the counter, held out your arms, and they started piling on the raincoat, overcoat, winter dress uniform, summer dress uniform, fatigue uniform, T-shirts, shorts, socks—everything the well-dressed soldier wears, and a duffel bag to pack it in.

We were still in the reception center, living in what I

34

first assumed were civil war barracks. And I was not alone in that assumption. At night we would stuff old newspapers in the holes in the walls to keep the wind out. After all, this was December. While we were out and about during the day doing our thing with the army, we all swore someone came in and removed all the papers and put out the fire in the furnace. When we returned to the barracks at night, it was an icebox.

We spent a week at the reception center. As raw recruits, we had to keep the top button on our shirts buttoned. This made us easy marks for harassment by more seasoned veterans. I also got my second command. We were lined up in formation in front of our barracks in the early morning darkness, waiting to go to breakfast. A sergeant came up to me and asked me our group number. "Group 64 I," I replied. He looked me in the eye and said, "You're about six foot four. March these men to the mess hall." I answered, "Yes, sir." And thanks to Mike Stengler and all of those hours of dismounted drill  during gym class, I pulled it off. I spent the months of December, January, and February taking basic training at Fort Dix, which I thought was located in New Jersey.  I was now convinced it was in the Hudson Bay area of Northern Canada. It was bitter cold.

I wasn't the Boogie Woogie Bugle Boy, but I was assigned to Company B, 1st Battalion, 272nd Infantry Regiment, 69th Infantry Division—the Fighting 69th, of both WW1 and WW2 fame.

The uniform of the day started with, of course, underwear, then woolen long johns, cotton socks, then woolen socks, fatigue uniform (in civilian life they are called work clothes), woolen OG shirt, field jacket with hood and insulated liner, fur hat, mittens, and finally—the real killer—overshoes (or what we used to call them, galoshes). Spend three months in that outfit and you'll probably be able to drive nails with your big toe.

The barracks that we now occupied were a big improvement over the reception barracks. We could no longer watch the moon come up or stargaze through the barrack walls, but that was a small price to pay for heat and hot water.

Our first night in our new home was pretty hectic. We were each issued one locker wall and one locker foot. That was the army's way of telling you that one locker will stand against the wall and the other at the foot of your bunk. We were all busy putting our new wardrobe away and getting ready to turn in. Lights were out at 2200 hours. That's 10:00 PM to you. With five commodes, six washbasins, and four showerheads, we had to develop a system. There were eighty of us in the barracks. The first night we got acquainted with each other. The army saw fit to house us alphabetically, starting with the A's in the first platoon. There are four platoons in an infantry company, and needless to say I ended up in the fourth platoon with all the S, T, U, V, and W's. There were no X's but a couple Y's and Z's.

I had always slept in my underwear, I guess since I was about five years old. And as I found out that night, so did about 90 percent of the male population. At least that was how it broke down in our little barracks world that night. When the 10 percent donned their PJs and house slippers, the 90 percent almost fell out of their bunks they were laughing so hard. It wasn't long before we were all snoring away in our army-issue boxer shorts and T-shirts.

0400 comes pretty early In the morning, , most of us were kids, just out of high school. We didn't have beards. We had cat whiskers, but the army says to shave every day, so here we were, half asleep, standing in front of a mirror with a razor blade in our hand, chasing a whisker around our face. Then it was a race to get dressed and ready to fall out for Reveille; In it's wisdom. the army issued us two pair of combat boots,which  we must alternate every day  , The army had us lace one pair with a cross lace and the other pair with a ladder lace. Today was cross lace day. One hurdle cleared, about two million to go.

When I joined the army, I was an eighteen-year-old kid. My experiences away from home could probably fit on the end of your pinky: summer Boy Scout camp and weekends working at Camp St. Regis. In Scout camp, if you had to answer the call of nature, you had the outdoor privy, or outhouse. Crude but private. Just you and the spiders, and maybe a snake or two. Out on Long Island, we had the big house—toilets, just like home. In the army we didn't have bathrooms. We had latrines, located at the end of the barracks on the first or ground floor. There were six washbasins five commodes, a shower room with four showerheads, and a urinal about five feet long. No matter how drunk you might be, there was no excuse to piss on your shoes. Also, forget about the only private room in the house being the bathroom. The days of the private solitary shit were over. You now had five bowls lined up shoulder-to-shoulder and one little low bowl reserved for those unlucky warriors hosting a herd of crabs.

It's amazing how quickly you adapt. Two weeks ago you were suppressing a public fart, and here you were now sitting side by side on the toilet discussing the previous day's events. The army was still new and strange to us, but we had communal shitting down pat.

In December 1955, "The Great Pretender" by the Platters was number one on the hit parade. We would go to the service club to relax after a full day of training, plus cleaning every mortar and cannon on Fort Dix, and listen to the very popular song over and over again. I would enjoy guilt-free smoking. My parents gave me permission to smoke when I was sixteen, but I could never bring myself to light up in front of them. Now I could smoke like a chimney without any guilt.

Volunteering is a nasty word, according to all the seasoned veterans. When informed I was about to join the army, the first piece of advice I received was to never, ever, volunteer. Chances were that you would end up on some shitty detail, and if you uttered one complaint, you would be reminded that you volunteered But I volunteered anyway as soon as I enlisted. What the hell. When they asked for a volunteer with the ability to drive a one-and-a-half-ton truck, I raised my hand. For a couple weeks I drove a meat truck for Mutual Provision, delivering corned beef and brisket to restaurants and butcher shops. I was qualified. "Step forward, Private." "Yes, sir," I barked, to which he barked even louder, "Don't 'sir' me, Private. Do you see bars on my shoulders?" "No, Sergeant!" I learned a lesson quickly and filed it away: Never insult a noncommissioned officer by addressing him as a commissioned officer. "Go with that corporal." I followed the corporal to the motor pool, where I was given a road test, which I passed, and told to report back to my formation, which I did.

We were all given a Christmas leave. I couldn't wait to get home to show off my new uniform. Of course, with no stripes on the sleeve, no piping on my cap, and no medals on my chest, the only thing separating me from the UPS driver was the "69th Infantry Division" on my left shoulder. Well, everyone told me how good I looked, asked if I was homesick and about the food—all the standard questions. As soon as Christmas was over, I couldn't wait to get back and start soldiering. I was wearing the uniform, but I hadn't even been issued a rifle yet.

That quickly changed. When we reported back to camp,

training started in earnest. I was issued a weapon, a Garand M1 30CAL gas-operated, clip-fed, semi-automatic rifle. When it was issued to me, it was literally thrown at me. Your name was called, you stepped forward, and this rifle came flying at you. You had better catch it. There you stood with this blue-steeled walnut-stocked beauty what a rush of adrenalin this is why was why you are here, You were now a member of the U.S. Armed Forces. Uncle Sam had enough confidence in you to give you a real weapon. My father wouldn't let me have a BB gun.

Of course, along with the rifle went sixty pounds of other assorted combat junk. Let's take a look at it: one steel helmet and liner, bayonet, entrenching tool (that's a shovel to you), and one shelter half with pegs and pole. Your partner has the other half of the tent and the other pole and pegs. You put them together and you have a two-man pup tent. There was also your canteen first aid kit, poncho, blanket, knapsack for your clean socks and underwear, ammunition, and don't forget hand grenades. You had to eat, so don't forget your mess kit and utensils. We were training in winter, so we also had to wear overshoes. Schlepping around in the ice and snow with all this junk on your back was no picnic, but it sure built up your stamina. After about four weeks, we started on the long hikes at 0400 and were back at 2100. All three meals were cooked and eaten in the field, and they were cooked in field kitchens, which were driven out to the field in ton-and-a-half trucks. Remember all that advice I received about not volunteering? You'll get all the shitty jobs. I had in my pocket a U.S. Army-issue driver's license for a ton-and-a-half truck. I threw all my junk into the back of the truck and drove the twenty miles to the bivouac area. I helped the cooks set up the kitchen. We drank coffee and waited for the marchers to show up. I didn't get out of all the hiking, but I got out of enough of them to make me feel as if I had beaten the system just a little bit.

Basic training was bad enough. In the winter it was terrible. Basic training was eight weeks long. Every day something was on the schedule. Weather delay was not in the army's dictionary. Rain or shine, the master schedule was faithfully followed I thought to myself, *My God, what did I set myself up for?* I didn't relish looking forward to three years of this.

KP was the worst. The advantage, of course, was that you got to work in a warm mess hall all day—and I mean all day, from 0300 to about 2100 hours. The night before your scheduled KP, you tied a towel to the foot of your bunk. At 0300 the CQ, or charge of quarters (he's the man who stayed up all night just to wake the KPs at 0300), would go through the barracks waking up the white towels. When you reported to the mess hall (in the army, no one ever "arrives at"; they "report to"), you were assigned to your job for that day. You may be the dining hall orderly, and you'd be responsible for the cleanliness and neatness of the dining hall. After every meal, the deck is mopped, tables are scrubbed, and the tables are set for the next meal. When you are finished, the cook inspects. You better hope that he doesn't find a solitary crumb or a grain of salt somewhere on the deck, or you will be doing it all over again. Neatness is next. We ate at four-man tables. Each table's condiments and napkins had to be perfectly lined up. When the inspecting cook squatted down at eye level with the tabletop and looked at that first table, he had better not see the second table, or the third, and so on. Everything had to be perfectly lined up, or else.

Or you may be the tray man, responsible for trays and silverware. They were run through an automatic dishwasher. The cook would give them the squeak test. He would rub his finger hard across the trays. If they squeaked, you were home free. If not, back they all went—hence the expression "squeaky clean." That sounded pretty easy, didn't it? It was, as long as the trays squeaked. There was also part two to the tray man job: garbage can cleaner. When a man finished his meal, he left the table and went outside, where he scraped his tray clean, putting napkins into the inedible can and food scraps into the edible can. These cans were emptied into trucks and carted away after every meal, and it was the responsibility of the tray man to restore these cans to their original pristine condition.

The next job was pot-and-pan man. That's self-explanatory. Again, all pots and pans were subject to the squeak test. You also peeled the potatoes, but the days of G.I. Joe sitting on a bucket next to a mountain of potatoes were over. The army had that job automated. We now used an electric peeler.

The absolute worst job was saved until the end. The army didn't plan it that way, but I'm sure they were happy it worked out that way. I'm talking about the grease trap. Anybody who ever served in any branch of the military knows about the grease trap. Every mess hall had one. The daily accumulation of kitchen grease had to be cleaned out of the trap before it got into the camp sewer system. After the cleanup of the last meal, we all went out and worked by the light of flashlights to clean out the grease trap then it was back to the barracks and into the sack , 4 a.m. comes very early in the morning

Basic training wasn't all bad. We had our lighter moments. As I mentioned before, sharing your bathroom with forty other men took some getting used to. So did sharing your bedroom. Picture an eighteen-year-old kid who recently left his own private bedroom now sharing a squad room with forty other men, all snoring and farting all night long. But you had to get used to it. I was looking at three years of army life.

At 0400 we were up and at 'em. We got dressed, fell in outside, went through the daily dozen, went back into the barracks to wash and shave our whisker, fell in for breakfast, and then like a bunch of seagulls, we raced back to the latrine and waited for a commode. At 0600 we fell out again, this time dressed for a day in the field, meeting that day's agenda. This went on for eight weeks, at the end of which I was again given leave. I was no longer a raw recruit. Now I was a basic infantry man, at least until I reported to my duty station in exotic Fort Eustis, Virginia.

I left Bayonne in early March 1956. It was nine degrees out, and I was dressed for it: long johns, overcoat, gloves, full winter outfit. I dragged my sixty-pound duffel bag on a bus and went to Penn Station in Newark, NJ, and caught a train to Washington, DC. There I switched to a Richmond, Fredericksburg, and Potomac train to Lee Hall, Virginia. I got off the train in the middle of nowhere. To make matters worse, the previous day I left Jersey. It was nine degrees. It was eighty-five here. I didn't have a clue as to how to get to Fort Eustis from here, so I asked somebody sitting at the station. I was told that a bus would come along shortly. It would take me there. It came and it did.

When I arrived at Fort Eustis, I knew it was the home of the Army Transportation Corps and the transportation schools, and that I was assigned to the Transportation Corps. When I reported in at the school, I was assigned to class 105, Harbor Craft Crewman School. I thought I died and went to heaven. I couldn't wait to get started.

Right away I noticed a big difference at Fort Eustis. Our days were much shorter. They still had twenty-four hours, but now we normally worked about eight of them at a time, except of course KP. That hung in there like the plague. I was an E-1 pay grade, and grades 1 through 3 did KP. I found out also that it didn't change any when you went to a different post. KP is KP. And it would take me two and a half years to make E-4.

I loved the army. I never had so much fun. We learned all the basic skills of a deck seaman: watch standing, boxing the compass, and marlinspike seamanship. We also spent a lot of time on the water. We stood watch, and we learned how to steer. Everything that we had learned in the classroom we practiced afloat. The last week of school we took a trip aboard an army freighter up to Philly, and on the way back we had a lifeboat drill. We rigged the cargo booms and ran the cargo winches. I loved it.

After graduation from seamanship school, I received my permanent duty assignment in Fort Story, Virginia. Where the hell was that? I found out that it was a satellite of Fort Eustis, located about twenty miles away at Cape Henry, right on the ocean. It was the Army's amphibious base. Except for two trips to the Arctic to supply DEW line bases, I would spend my three years at Fort Story.

I was assigned to the 554th heavy boat platoon as a deckhand on board a BARC, which stood for "barge, amphibious, resupply, cargo." I went aboard BARC 4X in the crew of a little redneck staff sergeant named Stillgrove from Jackson, Mississippi. The other crewmen were a deckhand from Panama named Pleasant and an engineer from Ohio named Byer. I arrived in time to go north with them. It was April 1956, and they were getting ready to leave for the Arctic. We got busy right away, overhauling equipment and packing spare parts and other gear.

Fort Story was, for lack of a better adjective, a nice post. It was located at Cape Henry, Virginia, right on the shores of the Atlantic Ocean on one side of the lighthouse and Chesapeake Bay on the other side. The first settlers landed there in the 1600s. It originally was a coast artillery installation guarding the entrance to the bay. The barracks were all of WWII vintage. My unit, the 554th, lived In building #1029, and we had it fixed up just like home. We chipped in and bought a TV set, a washing machine, and curtains for the windows. We also painted the interior a nice shade of green and varnished the floor. We kept it so nice that when we were sent overseas, the building was locked and off-limits to reservists, who normally occupied empty barracks while doing their mandatory two-week summer training.

The washing machine was a Maytag, with a hand crank wringer. It was a remarkable machine. Forty men constantly did their laundry day in and day out for the two and a half years that I was there, and that machine never skipped a beat. The Maytag repairman was truly the loneliest man in town.

We set aside a corner of the upstairs for a TV room, and every afternoon you would see us rushing back to the barracks to watch this new show, *American Bandstand*, hosted by a fellow by the name of Dick Clark. We all had our favorite girls who we watched for and made a fuss over. The all-time favorite of all of us, though, was Mouseketeer Annette Funicello. We'd all sit in front of the TV, some of us wearing Mickey Mouse hats, though I will say I never went that far.

By the end of June we were all ready to go. The boats were all tuned up and loaded with our equipment. All of our dress uniforms were packed and put away. We wouldn't need them in the Arctic.

We left in the beginning of July, right from Fort Story. The USS *Casa Grande*, LS.D.#13 anchored off the beach, she was a landing ship dock. They pumped water into her ballast tanks and sank her low enough in the water that we could just run the BARCs in. They pumped out the water. We chained everything down, and off we went to picturesque Frobisher Bay, Baffin Island, our home away from home for the next couple of months.

It took a couple of weeks to get there. Along the way, the *Andrea Doria* sank after being in a collision with the liner *Stockholm*. Quite a few lives were lost. We were kept informed over the ship's PA system, which also kept us up to date on the time zones. We went through about eight of them, usually around 2:00 AM.

The ship made a stop at Argentia, Newfoundland for bunkers. That's fuel to a landlubber. Argentia was—and I am sure still is—a pretty place, and the Newfies were a friendly people. Many years later I would be back to Newfoundland as a crewman on a merchant ship, and I liked them even more. You never had to count your change in a Newfie bar.

We couldn't wait to go ashore. For most of us this was our first time out of the country. As it worked out, I was one of the first to step on Newfoundland soil. I was picked to be a shore patrolman. I was given an armband and a billy club. What in hell they expected me to do with a billy club I didn't know. When you're six foot three inches tall and weigh in at 155 pounds, even with a billy club in your hand, you're not bullshitting anyone. But off I went. My first assignment was to ride the buses into town. That was a cakewalk. Everyone was in a good mood and anxious to get where the action was. After everyone was in town, I was stationed at the Gator Club, which was the navy-enlisted men's club. Unlike the army, where lowly privates can only buy beer, the navy will serve you hard liquor if you are twenty-one. My job was to check ages. No one underage would get in. I was just a week shy of turning nineteen, so I figured if he was nineteen, in he went. Everything was cool. There were no problems. The master at arms came by to check on things. He took my club and armband and relieved me for a couple hours to have some fun and see the sights. I told my relief how I was handling things, about the nineteen-year-old bit. He was a straight arrow from the word "go." I had to settle for a couple of 3.2 percent beers at the privates' bar.

I reported back at 2200, as ordered. It was back to the ship. Like I said before, the bus ride in was a breeze. The ride back to the ship was a hurricane, with all of these nineteen- and twenty-year-olds drunk as skunks. Disgraceful! Actually, the bus I was on wasn't bad. There were a couple puke jobs, which the driver (a huge navy third class) said he was used to. He told me there would be mops and buckets of water on the dock to handle situations like this. The following morning we said good-bye to Argentia and continued our northern trek.

A couple days out, we started to encounter ice, lots of it. We had two icebreakers with us, the USS *Edisto* and the USCG *Eastwind*. It was amazing to watch them work. They would go full speed up onto the ice and use their weight to break it. The ice would break with a noise akin to a cannon shot. The ice would open in front of the breaker, and she would then open the breach for us to follow. We had a navy seagoing salvage tug in our little convoy, put there in the event of a breakdown or other problem with one of the larger vessels. She, in fact, became the first casualty, being holed by a large piece of floating ice—or growler, as they were called. She had to drop out and go into Goose Bay Labrador for repairs. The rest of the convoy proceeded to Frobisher Bay.

We set up a tent city when we landed. Each BARC crew shared an eight-man tent, plus quarters for maintenance personnel and cooks, a mess tent, latrine, and last but not least a shower tent. It wasn't very cold when we arrived, but we knew that wouldn't last, so kerosene stoves were put in each tent. Later on we'd be wishing for two in the shower tent.

One of the strangest things we unpacked were mosquito nets. In the Arctic? A typical army snafu, you say? So did we. Until about the middle of August, when we were inundated with the biggest mosquitoes I had ever seen. And being from Bayonne, I thought nothing would match the size and tenacity of the Jersey mosquito, Bayonne division. For two weeks they ate us alive. Then as quickly as they arrived, they departed. Thank heavens.

We quickly got into our routine. Each crew worked twenty-four hours on and twenty-four hours off. We shuttled cargo from ship to shore around the clock. In August the air temperature was about forty-five degrees, and the water temperature was about twenty-seven degrees, so fog was a problem. But we had a radar picket boat that guided us from ship to shore by picking us up on radar and talking us in by radio. Most of the time it worked, but other times we would be running around in circles and they would come after us.

The run from shore to ship was about ten miles and would take us about two hours. Most of the loads we brought in consisted of 55-gallon drums of diesel fuel. We were capable of carrying 400 drums. Each weighed about 500 pounds. If you do the math, you're looking at 100 tons of cargo on each trip, and we did a lot of trips, four BARCs running around the clock for four months. We also carried other cargos. We delivered motor vehicles, food, and prefabricated housing for the Eskimos. The Canadian government was trying to move them out of igloos and tents into houses.

One Eskimo family celebrated their new digs by shooting a seal, bringing it into their brand-spanking-new

47

living room, and butchering it. What a mess. They moved them out to clean the place up and reeducate them.

One ship we unloaded was the *SS Goodwood*. A British freighter out of London built it in 1869, the same year that Bayonne was incorporated as a city. Part of her load was fiberglass insulation for the Eskimo housing, not exactly top priority. So she laid there for quite a while, and we got friendly with the crew. During one trip, a bag of insulation ripped open, showering me with the stuff. Man, does it itch! And you can't get it out of your clothes. One of the crew gave me a turtleneck sweater knitted by his mum from the wool of Highland sheep. It was the warmest sweater I ever wore. It lasted me thirty years before it just plain wore out, but it repelled water to the end. And when I worked on the tugs and barges, it served me well.

Of course we had the twenty-four–hour card games. BARC 3X's tent had a game going around the clock. People got in and out of the game as their shifts ended. 3X's crew managed to sleep through even the loudest games. I don't know how they did it. I guess it proved how hard we worked. I didn't do that well in the games. I love playing poker, but I can also read the writing on the wall, and the writing said, "Go to bed, and you'll wake up a richer man." So I did, and I did.

The weather grew progressively colder, and the days grew shorter, when we arrived. The sun never set. We were in the land of the midnight sun. As we got into October, the days were growing noticeably shorter. The cold turned showering from an exercise in personal hygiene to an Olympic event. We'd go in and take a nice hot shower. On the way back to our tents, our hair would freeze. One advantage of the shorter days was the fact that Sergeant Compton, the boat coxswain on my crew, was running out of excuses for not showering. "I only shower at night" was his lament. He now had plenty of it, and our tent smelled sweeter for it.

Ice was getting pretty thick in the harbor, and it was a real pain in the ass. We had to pick our way through it, and it turned a two-hour trip into a four-hour adventure. But we were almost done here. The ships were gone, and we started packing up—not to go home, though. We were on our way to Greenland, Sunderstrum Fjord, to be exact, for a small job and then onto Narsassarak Fjord.

We would not be returning on the good ship USS *Casa Grande*, very much to our dismay. Instead, we were embarking on the modern version of the *HMS Bounty*, the USS *Shadwell LSD #15*. Unlike the *Casa Grande*, they wanted to put us right to work chipping paint. As fast as the Bos'un issued us our chipping hammers, we threw them overboard. About four hundred hammers later, they finally got the message.

After a stop at Goose Bay Labrador and Argentia, Newfoundland, there was no shore patrol duty this time around, though. We headed home for Fort Story, and none too soon. Temperatures were dropping. Zero was common. We didn't want to get ice bound. Days were also getting shorter. There were just a couple hours of daylight per day now. One ship in our group, the USS *Lindenwald*, ran into some trouble on the east coast of Greenland. Half of our platoon was aboard her. She had to be towed into a sheltered fjord, where she eventually was locked in by ice. A navy tanker accompanying her removed the army troops and the civilian crew and took them to Goose Bay. They were flown back to the States. In the meantime, we were having our own problems. We ran smack into a hurricane. The ship changed course to go around the storm, but the storm just chased us, so we had to ride it out. And quite a ride it was. Sleeping was impossible. We were just thrown out of our bunks. The advantage was that the chow line was short. Back when I was nineteen, I had a pretty strong stomach. Later on in my life, when I sailed seagoing tugboats, I would look back on this storm with fond memories, not unlike a walk in the park. But for now this storm would do.

They had only one emergency. A chain securing one of the BARCs snapped, and she was banging against the side of the well deck. We had to go down there with sixty tons of sliding BARC and secure it before it went through the side of the ship. Actually, it wasn't all that hard to do. We shackled a new chain with a long turnbuckle and took the slack out of it before it snapped again. It held for the rest of the trip. The ship had its own problems. A pair of 40 mm antiaircraft guns, a couple of life rafts, and about fifty feet of railing were washed overboard, the weird thing, though, was going through the eye of the storm. The pressure was so low that you could feel it, and the ship had this slow lazy roll. I mean, she would almost dip her rails on every roll. We actually rolled a nickel on the deck from port to starboard. Before the nickel reached the starboard side, the ship would roll the other way and the nickel would roll back the other way. We kept that nickel rolling back and forth for quite a while. We eventually sailed back into the storm, and the wild ride started all over again. After that ride, Fort Story was a very welcome sight. We debarked offshore and made a mad dash for the beach. All of Fort Story was there to greet us, and we were glad to be home. After unpacking and taking care of the BARCs, we returned to garrison life, what we called soldiering—inspections, dismounted drills, parades, and a return to military courtesy, something that was kind of overlooked in the Arctic. When we meet a commissioned officer, we throw him a salute, which he is obligated to return.

If six of us spread out enough, he has to return six salutes. I'm sure he knew that was why we spread out.

Inspections were something that I could live without, especially something that we called Saturday morning junk on the bunk. Everything that you owned was put on display, on your bunk and in your lockers. Your personal clothing was displayed in your lockers. I owned socks and underwear that I never wore, for display purposes only. Your combat gear, rifle, bayonet, ammo clips, mess kit, etc., were laid out on your bunk. It usually happened once a month.

What I loved were dismounted drills. I loved marching and I loved taking charge and marching the platoon up to PFC. You were marched when you made corporal or specialist third class. You marched the troops. I could count cadence with the best of them. I had my hut 2-3-4, rear march, left flank, and right flank down to a tee. In fact, when I go for a walk to this day I take a thirty-inch pace. I do my cadence and delayed cadence count, and if I'm not counting, I'm singing "Stout-Hearted Men," our graduation song from St. Joseph's School.

There is nothing like a military parade to get the juices flowing. The band is playing, the flags are fluttering in the breeze, and the reviewing stand is awash in brass, waiting for us to pass in our tight little precision formation. The companies march by platoon when we are abreast of the stand. The platoon sergeant gives the command: "Eyes right!" And you could almost hear those eyeballs click. Of course we aren't looking at the reviewing stand. We're looking at the nose of the man on the right side of our line. You always want the man with the biggest nose in that position. As long as the rest of the line sees just the tip of his nose sticking out, they know that they're pretty much in line. All that aside, I still get chills when I hear a military band strike up. In fact, one of my favorite CDs is one of John Philip Sousa's collection of marching music.

I was very lucky in one respect, with a few exceptions. I served with a great bunch of guys. One of my good friends to this day is Kringo. We should have called him "Phone Book." His full name was Clinton Alyouis Ross Klondike Kringo Jr. We just called him kringo. Jim Thomas was known as Tommy Touch Hole, Ron Louis was Little Junior Looden, Lennox Brawn answered to Long Tall Ernest, and Bob Lang was just plain Ugmo. All of these nicknames were conferred by one Corporal Jonas. When Corporal Jonas was sober, he was one sharp soldier. When he was drunk, which was quite often, he was one funny comedian. He was busted so many times that he kept two sets of uniforms, one with corporal stripes and another with PFC stripes to save himself the trouble of all that sewing.

There were two other Jersey boys in my outfit. Bill Shalt was from Harrison, NJ. He was known to one and all as Zeke. Jim Callahan, a homeboy from Bayonne, was the only one to carry his nickname over from civilian life. I knew him from high school as Jumbo. He dubbed both Bill Shalt and myself with our monikers. He always called me Vagumpchik, due in part to most Irishmens' inability to pronounce anything Slovak or Polish. Well, Vagumpchik soon became Vagump. To further speed things up, Vagump became just plain Gump, and did it ever stick. I was soon known to one and all, officers and enlisted men alike, as just plain Gumps. On several occasions I saw myself listed twice on a duty roster. Up with the Gs I was Specialist Gumps, and down with the Vs I was Specialist Vargovcik. When I brought this up to the company clerk, he explained to me that, no, he was not acquainted with Specialist Vargovcik, but his name is on the platoon roster and he has to pull his weight with the rest of us. Of course he knew Specialist

Gump. "That's you," he said. "They're both me," I said. The problem was solved by shipping Vargovcik out.

The whole thing sounds as if it came right out of a Damon Runyon play, but after a while we actually had to think for a minute, to remember someone's given name. I would be remiss if I did not mention one more nickname, Lieutenant Mary (aka Lieutenant Sparborino). When she—whoops, there I go, I mean when he—was assigned to the unit, he was just bursting with enthusiasm. He was a second lieutenant fresh out of OCS. That's Officer Candidate School, where the army wanted me to go, and which I turned down, thankfully. He looked at us and saw a bunch of sad sacks. We wore ankle-high work shoes instead of the usual combat boots with bloused pants. And instead of the standard blocked Ridgeway cap, we wore a soft fatigue cap. She was going to change all of this and whip us into shape. The lieutenant was fast becoming a chickenshit officer, and they usually don't last long. We gave him a hard time, and he was constantly bringing someone up on charges of one kind or another, but there were never any witnesses to support his charges and they were always dropped as was Lieutenant Sparborino He was transferred out and was never heard from again. He was replaced by Lieutenant White, who was well liked and respected and had a much easier time of it. In fact, he would be our CO for a while.

Far and away the best officer I served under in my three years was Chief Warrant Officer Tony Zinc. He was not a commissioned officer and technically could not be our commanding officer, but he was well liked and respected, and we would do anything he asked of us. So the higher-ups left him in charge, and we were all the better for it.

I will tell one story that will explain why we thought so highly of him. I left for home on a weekend pass. I got a ride up to exit 14 on the Jersey Turnpike. I was going to walk over to Newark Airport and get a bus. The toll collector offered to get me a ride to Bayonne. "You'll be home in fifteen minutes instead of two hours on the bus." It made sense to me. As luck would have it, the only offer of a ride was from a state trooper, who picked me up for hitchhiking. I told him about the toll collector's offer, but to no avail. I was busted, especially after I looked at his name tag, which read "Cooper." I can't believe I said, "Well, Trooper Cooper, what now?" Next thing I knew, I was in a paddy wagon under the care of armed forces, on my way to New York City. I asked if I could be dropped off in Bayonne, but they had other plans for me. I told them about my stints in the shore patrol in Argentia, Newfoundland, figuring a little professional courtesy may be in order. No dice. It was off to the big city. The name "Big Apple" hadn't been coined yet. When we arrived in New York, they pulled my weekend pass and issued me an eight-hour pass, just enough time to get me back to Fort Story and file a notice of a delinquency report. I immediately went home for the rest of the weekend. From there I called our orderly room at Fort Story and explained the situation to Sergeant Rodgers, our first sergeant. He told me that he would leave a blank space in the sign-in book to coincide with my required arrival time. He also told me to enjoy the weekend and don't get picked up for anything else or I would be in big trouble. And he would see me at Monday morning formation.

I enjoyed the weekend at home and returned to Fort Story with no further incident. I found the allotted space in the sign-in book, I signed in, and I was home free. About three months later I was told to report to the maintenance shop office, where Mr. Zinc normally held court. "Gumps, have you ever been in any trouble in your short military career?" "No, sir," I replied. "Well, you still aren't." And with that, he handed me the delinquency report sent down from

New York, along with a list of appropriate actions he could take against me. "Tear it up and file it in that little round filing cabinet in the corner." "Yes, sir, and thank you, sir." And that was that. Record intact.

I was transferred from BARC 4x over to BARC 2x. I was glad to make the move. Old Sergeant Sllgrove could be a real pain in the ass, especially when he was drinking, which was pretty much most of the time. My new crew chief was a sergeant first class by the name of Utracht. He was a very easygoing sort, well liked by everyone. He was going through a divorce at the time and was living in the barracks. Sergeant. Utracht had one—I guess you could say—talent. He was a farting machine. On request at any time he would cut one loose. He was so good, in fact, that during dismounted drills he would count cadence with expelled flatulence. Far and away his was the most talented gastrointestinal tract we had ever seen, or rather heard. But as I said, he was pretty easy to get along with, and 2x was a happy boat.

Then there was the episode with the prisoner and Sergeant Utracht. We had a prisoner being held over the weekend by the name of Marchall. He was caught passing bad checks. We were guarding him until the civil cops came for him on Monday. He was under the guard of Jim North. Jimmy was a good old boy from DC and liked to party. He felt sorry for Old Marchall. He said that where he was probably going he wouldn't be able to drink, so they both went down to the beer hall, .45 caliber pistol and all. A couple of hours later, here came North and Marchall. North was shitfaced, and Marchall was practically carrying him and was wearing the .45 pistol. We weren't worried about Marchall using the pistol. He explained that it was easier to wear it than try to carry both it and North. We told both of them to go back to the orderly room, where they belonged, and leave us to our TV. They both got to arguing. Marchall wanted to go back to the orderly room, where he belonged, and North wanted to watch TV. The argument turned to ballistics, .45 caliber ballistics in fact. North claimed that he could run the length of the barracks and be down the stairs before Marchall could chamber a round, aim, and fire. Before he could react, North was off and running. Marchall picked up the pistol, chambered a round, aimed, and fired. North won. He was long gone. The round went through the wall by the stairwell and through the wall to Sergeant Utracht's room. He had been lying on his bunk reading a paper. He was covered with splinters, plasterboard, and his newspaper. "What the hell are you all up to now?" was all that he said after we cleaned up his room and repaired the damage to the walls. We told him what happened. His comment was that it was too bad Marchall wouldn't be around long. He would teach him to be faster on the draw.

One little comment: I've been heard to use the expression "hotter than a two dollar pistol on the fourth of July. Jim north used it a lot. I just picked up on it.

I'll relate another shooting incident. This one involved good old Corporal Jonas. Daniel Boone, he ain't. There were ten vertical supports in the barracks. They held up the second floor we hung #10cans half full of water.on them, When you finished a cigarette ,that was where it was supposed to go—a fire prevention thing. It was 2:00 AM. In came Corporal Jonas, drunker than a skunk. He plopped his ass down on the first foot locker he came to and took aim at one of the butt cans. Who knew which one—there where ten of them, and he probably was seeing twenty. And blast away. Every body hit the deck, even on the second floor, which was where I slept. There was silence and then blam, blam. Two more shots and then a door slammed. Everybody was still hugging the deck. Blam, blam, blam.

Three more shots, outside this time. We all ran downstairs to see what the hell was going on. Someone put the lights on, and the butt cans were all in good shape, with no holes in them. But wait a minute. There were two holes in the water fountain. What the hell was going on? If Twenty Pennies, which was Corporal Jonas's nickname, borrowed twenty cents from you, you'd forget it by payday, but five mooches would net him a buck, a princely sum when you were making four bucks a day. Somebody saw him come into the barracks, sit down on the foot locker, and light up a cigarette. The next thing we knew all hell broke loose. Then we all went outside to see what he did. There we found him sitting in a car he had borrowed. He forgot to roll up the window, and it had rained, quite hard in fact. The car was flooded, so he shot three holes in the floor to let the water out. We accounted for five shots. He had a six shooter. We went back in the barracks to look for it, and we found it in Gerry Gilman's locker—or rather through his locker, and half of his uniforms. We hushed it up. A piece of tape covered the hole in the locker, and Twenty Pennies swore he would pay for Gilman's uniforms, which he did. We often wondered how many people he hit up for twenty cents to pay him back.

One more gun story involved two black soldiers, Corporal Dumas and Private Alvin. Dumas was a career man, and there was no other way to describe Alvin than to call him a fuckup. He didn't give a rat's ass about anything or anybody. He didn't like the army or anything to do with the army, and he wasn't a draftee. He upped and joined of his own free will.

Payday came around once a month in the army. The first of the month the eagle shit, everyone was rich, and there was always somebody waiting to take it. Corporal Dumas would get a game of blackjack going among the blacks. He was always the bank or dealer, his rationale being that he could add faster than they could, so the game would be faster and he would get their pay faster. It was fascinating to watch him in action. He'd be sitting there with a ten and a seven showing. Everyone else would have at least a picture card showing. He had to take a hit. He would turn up a six, ten, seven, and six. He'd holler "twenty-one," and he'd rake in the money and the cards so quickly that they couldn't do the math. He would do this time and time again. Once in a while he would let someone else win just to make it look good. In the meantime they would be shaking their heads and proclaiming Dumas the luckiest man God ever put breath in.

Private Alvin sat down to try his luck, and it was as bad as everyone else's. But Alvin was smarter than the average bear. He didn't buy it. He called Dumas on it and, just like in the old West, the chairs went flying, and the footlocker they were playing on also went sailing across the room. Alvin pulled out a knife. "Fight like a man," Dumas chided him, so Alvin threw the knife away. Big mistake. Alvin was no heavyweight. He could probably take a nap on a two-by-four. They went at it, and pretty soon Dumas was straddling Alvin's chest. He pulled out a .32 pistol, pointed it at Alvin's head, and pulled the trigger—not once, but five times, and missed every time. When Alvin looked up that gun barrel, he went berserk, rolling his head from side to side and kicking and squirming. Between that and the fact that Dumas forgot the most basic rule of marksmanship—squeeze, do not pull the trigger—they both got up and ran in opposite directions. Dumas later remarked that he would have been justified in shooting Alvin because he pulled a knife on him. The most amazing thing about the whole affair was that before the paint dried on the new pieces of flooring that we put in to cover it up, Alvin and Dumas were arms-around-each-other buddies.

Our trip to the Arctic in 1957 was cancelled, so we were resigned to spending the summer at Fort Story, where the temperature and the humidity ran neck and neck. One thing the army didn't give us was air-conditioning. I had broken my finger playing first base on the company team, so I might not have gone anyway. I spent six weeks as barracks orderly, until they removed the cast. I was never so glad to see anything go as I was to see that cast come off. It was so hot, and I sweat like hell, which caused my hand to itch under the cast. I carried a coat hanger around with me so I could use it to reach under the cast and scratch my itches.

Near the end of the summer of 1957, the new BARCs started arriving—5, 6, 7, 8, and 9. I was assigned to number seven. I was a PFC. I was promoted in January 1957, but I still didn't have enough rank to hold down the assistant crew chief job on a permanent basis. Sergeant Jones had the job on paper, but he was a good carpenter, and he liked it, so he continued to do that job and I continued to hold down the assistant job despite the objections of a couple of lifers a who thought I was infringing into their territory.....

Preparations were under way for another deployment to the Arctic. This time it was going to be Thule,Greenland, One very cold place, six months of daylight didn't do much to warm it up

Instead of the tents that we lived in at Frobisher Bay, here we lived in aluminum barracks four men to a room,it was pretty comfortable even in the coldest weather and because of the weather we had a unique plumbing system, three large tanks, one tank held potable water, for drinking and showering and tank #2 held grey water from the showers and wash basins. That water was used to flush the toilets from there it went into the septic tank, when it was near full a truck was called to pump it out. We always took the unit, numbers of those trucks to make sure they didn't come to fill our potable tank.

Operating conditions were good , calm water and short runs from ship to shore and very little fog. Water temperatures were a little on the chilly side in the high 20's ,you would not last long in that water in fact we had a deckhand fall overboard and according to the report they got him out so fast his underwear was still dry?

In June 1958 I was promoted to specialist third class, an E-4 pay grade one under E-5, good enough to be permanently assigned as an operator on BARC 7. As a specialist third class my authority was limited to my specialty, which was boat coxswain, but when I was running my boat I outranked a general, so they say. I had generals on board, but I never put it to the test. The highest-ranking passenger I ever had on board was the prime minister of Denmark. Hansen was his name. I was pretty nervous about taking him and his party out for a tour of the harbor in Thule, Greenland. But after a few minutes of conversation, I found him to be very down-to-earth. He asked me my age. I had just turned twenty-one. He wished me a happy birthday. When I told him my name, he knew right away—a Slovak. A lot of pictures were taken, and I was promised a set, but I never did get them. I should have pursued the issue, but when I got out of the army, I kind of put it on the back burner. When Judy and I started raising a family, I started thinking how great it would be to have these pictures to show my kids. I went over to the Danish consulate in New York, but they couldn't or wouldn't help me. I didn't know which, but I never got my pictures.

One particular incident that struck a sour note with me happened in Thule, Greenland. It happened around September or October. Because it was bitter cold, about six or eight of us were in one of the bunk rooms playing poker.

During the course of the game, Lieutenant White stuck his head in the room to say hello. It was a very relaxed momentt until Sergeant Grambler stuck his nose into it. When the lieutenant came into the room, the first man to see him should have called us to attention. Nobody did. Since I was the ranking man in the room, I was called on the carpet. Sergeant Grambler complained, so First Sergeant Allard had to do something about it. I was told to round up everyone who was in the room and fall out for four hours of dismounted drills—that's marching, for the uninitiated. There is nothing that I like better than to march a bunch of soldiers, but not in ten-degree weather, amid a lot of grumbling. We got it done. Sergeant Allard called us into the orderly room, where he had hot coffee waiting for us. He offered us a ride back to our barracks, but I graciously declined. I told him that we would walk. It would be good exercise.

One advantage to serving in a God forsaken place like Thule is that you go to the top of the list for the USO shows. We never heard of any of the acts. They were all wannabes, but they were pretty good. It was as cold as it could be, around zero degrees outside and not much warmer inside. We all sat there with our parkas on, but the girls were up there with their skimpy costumes and gowns and goose bumps, singing and dancing their hearts out. We loved it. The Bob Hope Christmas Show appeared at Thule that year, but we left before they arrived.

Unlike our previous trip back from the Arctic, we had beautiful weather all the way home. Unlike in 1956 when we unloaded right off the beach at Fort Story, this time we unloaded in the harbor of Norfolk. We had a six-hour trip by water back to Fort Story. We arrived late that night, and the people waiting for us on the beach had vehicles parked with their headlights on to guide us in. We found out later that the reason we debarked at Norfolk was that four

BARCs were already loaded aboard a ship, waiting to leave for the island of Formosa, and they were going to transfer all of our spare parts and equipment to that ship. Formosa was a big trouble spot at that time. Communist China was shelling the island and threatening to invade, so the United States was reinforcing the nationalist Chinese, and the four BARCs were part of that buildup. Six members of the platoon who didn't have enough time left on their hitch to make the trip to Greenland found themselves looking at a six-month extension and a trip to China in letters that we received from them. They weren't too upset about it. It turned out to be good duty.

I was getting short-timer cramps big time. I was down to one month to go. Decision time. I loved the army. I loved what I was doing. Do I re-enlist or do I get out? I joined the army at the age of eighteen. I was now twenty-one and a lot wiser. I missed my family, but not to the point that I was ever homesick. I know that my mother missed me and worried about me, but I wrote home often, and if I could I called once a week. I did make it home every Christmas. I decided to get out and try civilian life as a twenty-one-year-old. If I didn't like it, I had ninety days to reenlist and hold my rank. Big mistake, I should have just stayed in. Once I got out, I went back to work at the Maidenform Brassiere Company, where they offered me an apprenticeship as a tool and die maker. I took it and immediately hated it. I was used to being outdoors. I was now stuck inside a machine shop for eight hours.

Then I started hanging around again with Jimmy Slick and John Stoffic. They were out of the Marine corps, but I never held it against them. We started hanging out at a place called the Venice. It was a bar and pizza parlor. It had a back room with a juke box and lots of girls.

# CHAPTER 8: CUPID DOES A ROBIN HOOD

In July 1960, something happened that would change my whole life, though I didn't know it at the time. I was introduced to Judy Lach. I liked her right from the first time I met her, though at the time it was just as a friend. But every time I came to the Venice alone, I would look for her car parked outside. When I went in I would look to see where she was sitting, and I would spend the evening with her. I enjoyed her company.

Two years later, my friend Jim Slick was getting married to Carol Lorton. I was asked to be an usher in the wedding party. I was glad when I found that my partner would be Judy Lach. It would be quite the day. She looked beautiful in her gown, and there I was in my rented tux. I thought that we made a nice couple. We didn't know it yet, but that was the first day of the rest of our lives. We have been together ever since.

On our first date we went to a movie starring Jeff Chandler, named *Broken Arrow*. The movie was so-so, but the company was great. It was playing at the old state theater on Journal Square in Jersey City. Unlike today, back then it was a safe place to go.

The Slicks returned from their honeymoon. We paid

them a visit in their new apartment down on West Third Street. It was in the attic of a two-family house, way up there in nosebleed country. By the time we climbed all those stairs, we needed a drink, and Jimmy was always glad to oblige. One thing he always had plenty of was beer. They regaled us with tales of connubial bliss and the delights of cohabitation. Jimmy was sitting there with this big shitty grin on his face, and Carol was sitting so close to him you couldn't put a dime between them. They painted a pretty picture of married life. Of course they left out Carol's aversion to cleaning toilet bowls or the fact that Jimmy's used handkerchiefs went not into the washing machine but into the garbage. But all that aside, they did look genuinely happy.

After less than two months of dating, I proposed. By now I felt as if I had known Judy all of my life. I wanted to be with her for the rest of it. I did not get on bended knee to propose. I proposed in the front seat of my Chevy. Judy accepted, and I was on cloud nine. We announced our betrothal on March 17, St. Patrick's Day. I don't really know why we picked that day, since neither one of us was Irish. I needed time to buy a ring, and Christmas was too close. I wanted the ring to be special for a special girl. We let the whole world know about our upcoming marriage—well, the Bayonne part of the world anyway. We set the date for May 2, 1964. That would be a very long fourteen months.

The next year was spent doing all the things engaged couples do. We went furniture shopping and apartment hunting. We reserved a hall for our reception and lined up a photographer and a florist. Then, of course, there was the wedding gown. Judy wanted to be just so, and she was a very beautiful bride.

We rented a three-room apartment at 46 east Eighteenth Street. It was newly renovated. I had worked on putting the heating system in, so I had an inside track. Good apartments were hard to come by. The rent was eighty bucks a month, and heat and hot water were supplied.

We saw an awful lot of each other during those fourteen months. I was working the afternoon shift, driving a truck in New York City. I usually got off at about eleven or twelve at night. I would catch a bus for the one-hour trip back to Bayonne. Judy waited up for me so that we could spend an hour together every night. If I didn't see her one night, she would come to my house the next morning, tiptoe up the back stairs, and wake me up. We didn't miss a day.

While all of this was going on, we still had a wedding to plan. Judy's sister Carol was the maid of honor, and Joanne was a bridesmaid, along with Carol Slick and Carol Florky. Jimmy Slick was my best man. My cousins Charles Danko, Frank Barone, and Frank Carter were ushers.

Those fourteen months were flying by. The next thing I knew, it was shower time. It was held at Hendrickson's Restaurant on Thirty-First Street and Broadway. Lots of women were there, all friends and relatives, and we received a lot of great gifts.

May 2 finally arrived. Judy and I were not getting married at mass, so we attended a morning mass. Then I took her home. I wasn't supposed to see her again until we were in church to be married.

Everybody was a nervous wreck that day, except me. I was as cool as a cuke. Why should I be nervous? I knew exactly what I was getting into, and I couldn't wait. I wanted Judy for my wife forever!

It was a great day for my mother. She was finally seeing her son get married. My father was beaming. My parents both thought the world of Judy, and they were very happy for me.

The reception was held at the MacKenzie Post American

Legion Hall. There were about 150 guests. We fed them all chicken and kielbasa and gave them unlimited booze. Carl Kula and his Fabulous Five provided the music. We had a great time; in fact, they had to throw us out the door so we could start our honeymoon.

We honeymooned in Florida. We drove down in my—or should I say our—1960 Chevy. The Chesapeake Bay Bridge Tunnel opened the previous day. It was brand-spanking-new when we went through. I made a stop at Fort Story, VA, the base I was stationed at in the army. It was the first time that I was back there since getting discharged in 1958. I met my old first sergeant when I visited the orderly room. I was in there so long that Judy thought I had reenlisted. I took her down to see the BARCs and give a quick tour of the base. We stayed at a motel in Virginia Beach that was right on the ocean. We fell asleep listening to the sound of the ocean.

The next morning we resumed our trip. There was no I-95 back then. It was Route 17 all the way to Florida. We stopped at St. Augustine to see the Fountain of Youth. We took a drink. It didn't work. We drove on the beach in Fort Lauderdale, something that you can't do anymore. Cape Canaveral was just sand dunes, no rockets yet. We looked at ocean front property in Flagler Beach that cost $17,000. These people were crazy.

Those two weeks flew by. The trip was over but not the honeymoon. That's a work in progress. We just keep adding onto it.

We settled into our apartment on East Eighteenth Street. I didn't have to be in work until noon. Judy, on the other hand, had to be in at 8:00—that's AM. The first morning that Judy had to return to work, I figured I would get up and make her some breakfast. I did it once and found out that Judy was not one for niceties in the morning. It was best to just stay out of her way. I have been working on her, though, and I must say that over the years, she has mellowed considerably.

Stanley and Steffie were our landlords on Eighteenth Street. They were a very nice couple but a little weird. Stanley would go to the corner saloon early in the morning when they were cleaning up from the previous night's revelry and get the early edition of the daily news, which by now was in the trash can. The news was a little old, but he saved twenty cents. The man didn't work. His job was to take care of the house. Steffie was the breadwinner, sewing ladies' undergarments at the petticoat factory. But Stanley did a good job. The house was spotless and well maintained, but hot. The house had a flat roof, and we lived on the top floor, with no air-conditioning. I came home from work one night to find Judy cleaning the floors, clad only in a bra and panties. I thought it was very sexy. She wasn't hearing any of that. She was just too damn hot to wear clothes. She said that we needed air-conditioning. I told her that she looked great without it. I didn't think the wiring in the old house would have handled it. Anyway, it was a moot point. Judy became pregnant with Krissy, and we were looking for larger quarters to handle a growing family. We packed and moved to 34 Humphries Avenue. We had four rooms in a nice little 2family house located between Second and Third Streets. It was in a really nice neighborhood. Stella was our very nice landlady, who also had a wacky son.

I was working nights at the time, driving tractor trailers for the Railway Express Company over in New York. I enjoyed taking Kris for walks down on First Street. We would watch the boats go by, and I would daydream about one day being aboard. This was 1965, and I would have a long time to wait. We enjoyed living there. My mother's brother, Uncle Richie, my aunt Irene, and my cousin Theresa lived across the street from us at 27 Humphries

Avenue. They were a help for Judy with Kris. Theresa had five daughters. Theresa's husband, Joe, and I occasionally went next door to the corner bar, Chris's Corner, for a couple of beers. Life was good. The proverbial monkey wrench was thrown into the works in 1967. My mother became very sick. She was never running at 100 percent as it was, but she was a great person, and I loved her dearly. I know that she worried about me when I was growing up and when I was away in the army for three years. I know that when I married Judy, she heaved a big sigh of relief,. Mission accomplished. When Krissy was born, that was the icing on the cake. But this was the big one. My sister and I didn't know how sick she really was until the doctor called us into his office and laid it all out. He gave her six months to live. This was April 1967. She died on June 14. He was off by four months.

My mother had a very big funeral. There were at least thirty cars in the procession. She would have been very happy with that. She loved a fuss. I was always very close to my mother, and I missed her very much. I still do.

Judy was pregnant at the time, and we had to take my father in to live with us. So we moved again, this time to 156 West Twenty-First Street, down by Newark Bay. Elsie and Bill were our landlords. They were very nice people, and Elsie loved to babysit for us. My father enjoyed living there. At my aunt's house he was on the second floor and couldn't get out too often because of the stairs. Here he was on the first floor and could walk down to Basile's Tavern on the Bay, have a beer, and watch the boats go by. Not long after that, he lost his leg to gangrene. That ended his outings to Basile's. About a year and a half later, he lost his other leg. He never came home again. He went to a rehab. Then Judy became pregnant with Robbie. My father needed professional care at this point, so the doctor advised that he stay in the nursing home. It was a very tough decision, but we could not provide the twenty-four–hour care that he needed. My father was a hard worker all of his life. He was a boatman. I followed in his footsteps. He was a captain for Dalzell Towing. When they sold the boat to Esso, he went with it. When Esso sold the boat to Nelson Transportation, he again changed companies and went with the boat. Nelson went out of business in 1942, and he went back to Esso, where he worked on the *Esso Charlie White* until 1950, when it was sold and replaced by the newly built lighter *Esso Dispatch*. He retired in 1958. He never really had much of a retirement. His health just went downhill until he died in May 1971. He was seventy-four. I took some criticism from his sisters about his staying in the nursing home. But on the rare occasion that they came to visit him, they never stayed long or brought a little something for him, so I took it for the bullshit that it was.

Nancy was born on August 17, 1967, two years and one week after Kris. I was an old hand at having babies by now, so when Judy said, "Let's go," I figured there was no rush. I took her into the hospital in the morning for Kris, and she wasn't born until the afternoon. We left the house at 5:00 AM. I dutifully stopped for all the traffic lights and arrived at the hospital at 5:25. Nancy was born at 5:30. In fact, they got Judy to the delivery room barely in the nick of time.

I was humbled by that experience. That was too close for comfort. If I had to do it again, I would not be so flippant about the whole thing. I wasn't when Robbie was born three years later. We were there with plenty of time to spare. When Robbie was born, our family was complete, two girls and a boy.

Nancy was born two months after my mother died. It was a busy time for us. We moved from Stella's house on Humphries Avenue to Elsie's house on West Twenty-First

Street. My father moved in with us, and I was starting a new job driving a truck for Metropolitan Petroleum, delivering heavy black oil to factories and large office buildings. It was a good-paying job with good benefits, so I jumped at it.

# CHAPTER 9: JOBS

Since my discharge from the army in 1958, I've had a few jobs. I went back to Maidenform for a while. Then I worked out of Union Hall in New York as an oiler.and deckhand on tugboats. The jobs were few and far between, so I had to give it up and get a steadier job. I went to work for Beacon Oil in Bayonne. I delivered home heating to houses in Hudson, Essex, and Union Counties. I was paid two and a half mils per gallon, or a buck and a half an hour, whichever was greater If I delivered 10,000 gallons a day I would make a cool 25 bucks I worked there until December 1960. Then I schlepped over to New York City, where I got a job driving a delivery truck for the Railway Express Company. The pay was better there. I grossed $98.80 without overtime, which was plentiful, so I was making a pretty good buck. Then I was laid off. They called for a reduction in force. Either way I was out of a job. Back to Beacon Oil. I guess they liked me. They took me right back, but I always gave them a good day's work. I stayed there until Railway called me back in late 1961. Beacon Oil wasn't happy, but the money in New York was too good to pass up. I was now knocking down $108.80 a week. The job also had its interesting moments. I once met Joan Crawford, the actress, when I delivered her fur coats to her apartment. I also met Della Reese when

I delivered to her apartment. The job had its moments. I loved working at night. New York at night was a whole different place. There were the day people, and then there were the night people. I liked the night people better. I started driving tractor trailers in 1964. I had to get a New York Class 1 driver's license to meet the requirements. They didn't recognize New Jersey licenses.

Trailer drivers didn't make deliveries, not at Railway Express (or REA Express, as it was now called). We drove terminal to terminal and to the railroad piggyback yards. The job was a snap, and again the money was great. I had a run for a while, called a westside tripper. We pulled twenty-foot trailers between two terminals: Thirty-Third Street and Tenth Avenue, and Sixteenth Street and Ninth Avenue both on the west side of Manhattan. We were given one hour to make the round-trip. We easily did it in twenty minutes, but we took the hour on paper so that I would do eight rounds. It would take me four hours, but my trip card showed eight hours. If I started at 4:00 PM, my paperwork showed that I now had my eight hours in and I could go home. Or I could be greedy and keep going, doing eight more rounds and making four hours of overtime, at time and a half. I was greedy. The thing was that the company knew all about it, but they looked the other way, because the Thirty-Third Street terminal was a dinosaur from the horse-and-wagon days. Twenty-foot trailers were the biggest it could handle. On the other hand, the Sixteenth Street terminal was fully automated. The twenty-foot trailers were loaded and unloaded in minutes. If we didn't hustle like we did, trailers would be backed up all the way to Thirty-Third Street. So management had to look the other way while we screwed 'em. Me? I laughed all the way to the bank.

But all good things must come to an end, and so did REA Express. They eventually went under, but it wasn't my fault. The government raised the size and weight limits on parcel post, putting them head-to-head with REA. There was no contest. At that time the post office did not have to show a profit. REA did. End of story.

It was now 1966. I was offered a job at Tidewater Associated Oil Company, known today as Getty Oil. I jumped at it. I got the job through the owner of a heating oil company in Bayonne, by the name of John Zeintle. He heard that they were looking for drivers, so he recommended me, and I was hired in the fall of 1966. Again it was night work. I worked four ten-hour days, Monday, Wednesday, Friday, and Saturday. To me it seemed as if I was always off. Judy wasn't too crazy about the Saturdays. At REA I worked Saturdays, but like I mentioned earlier, I started at four and was home a little after eight. Here I started at four, but I didn't get home until the wee hours of the morning.

Christmas of 1966 was a disaster. I went in early on Christmas Eve day in order to finish earlier, but as luck would have it, we were in for a white Christmas, a very white Christmas. I remember my trip. It was a snap, two drops, the Yonkers, NY Police station, and a taxi cab garage. I should have been home in plenty of time to lay the carpet that was going to be delivered that day and trim the Christmas tree. It was not to be.

Back then the Jersey Turnpike was nothing like it is today. Route 80 wasn't finished, and the pike ended at Ridgefield Park, when you crossed the GW Bridge. You traveled on Route 46 to a jughandle to get on the pike. There was a blizzard. I was now empty, so I lost a lot of my traction, but I was doing fine. From here I figured an hour tops to Newark. We were traveling single file with only one lane open in each direction. I entered the jughandle for the pike with a farm boy from North Carolina in front of me and a couple of trailers behind me. Three-quarters of the way around the loop, guess who runs out of gas: farm boy. I was pulling a gas tanker, but I didn't have even a cup on board. Believe me, I tried every hose and every valve. Not a drop. My tractor was a diesel. No help there. I told myself, "This is shaping up to be a long night." It was.

I finally rolled in Christmas morning. I walked in the front door and tripped over the rolled up carpet in the front hall, delivered on time in a blizzard. Unbelievable. Judy and I put down the rug and decorated the Christmas tree. I then settled down for a short winters nap.

Then it was off to Judy's moms house for Christmas Dinner with the family.

My career at Tidewater didn't last long.. I was there about two months when I rear-ended a truck owned by M&M Transportation. It wasn't bad, just a tap. "No problem," the driver assured me. That was until he got back to his terminal. Somebody talked to him, and he now was suffering from whiplash and a back injury. Tidewater checked out the truck, and the driver on the previous day didn't drain the air tank, and the water froze. The result was no brakes. They called it mechanical failure, but that would have a negative effect on the insurance, so I had to go. But they gave me a good recommendation. Then I really messed up. I bought my own truck, a 1958 B61 Mack with a 238 hp engine and a nine-speed duplex transmission. I went to work for Eastern of New Jersey, a fairly good-size fuel oil company. I delivered to apartment houses and factories. The money was good as long as the truck was running, but I had a couple of breakdowns, and they liked to kill me. I was not comfortable driving my own truck. When I broke down, I just wanted to drop a dime and wait for a mechanic. With my own truck, I was on my own. And I didn't have enough money to carry me through a major repair.

In December 1967 I went to work for Metropolitan Petroleum down at Tank Port terminals in Jersey City. It was one of the best jobs I ever had, money- and benefit-wise. I was there three months, and at the end of winter, layoff was staring me in the eye. But lo and behold my uncle Rich got me a job at Humble Oil, known today as Exxon. I said to myself, "Bob, your day has finally come." My dentist, old Dr. Kasko, once told me that if you worked at Esso, you could marry anybody's daughter. If nothing else, it was an eye opener for me. I never saw so much backstabbing and bad-mouthing in all of my life.

I worked in what they called the Greer Building. It was the wax division, and we molded the wax into eleven-pound slabs to be packed into boxes. I drove a forklift in the shipping department, and I worked the packing line. Then an assistant operator job opened up on the molding machine. Nobody wanted it. It paid a dollar an hour more. I jumped at it. I got the job. Now everybody wanted it. I was dropped back to utility man.

I have to tell you there was a little drama involved here. Back in 1958 there was a big layoff in the refinery. A lot of men lost their jobs. Uncle Frank was one of them. In 1959 Esso closed down the marine service department. That was where my father worked. He retired, but the rest of the men from that department were sent to the refinery. The laid-off men were never called back. They were off for more than a year. It caused a lot of hard feelings among the old refinery hands. Ten years later, it was pointed out to me that my father worked in the marine department, and I was not welcome there. I told them that they could take their job and shove it.

I went to work for Matlack Transportation, running chemicals over the road. That was in 1970. In August 1972, I was back at Metropolitan Petroleum. I would stay there until 1979.

Henry "Digger" O'Dell was one of the yardmen at the terminal, and he had a friend named Juan Alcadoro. Juan owned four tugboats and owed Digger money. Digger made a phone call, and I've been in the boat business ever since. I was discharged from the army back in 1958. I had been trying to get a job on the water. Finally! I started out as a hammer. I worked for nothing until a job opened up and I got into the union. In the meantime, I was learning the ropes. I would meet the good tug *Julian A.* on Friday night. I had to chase her to wherever she was. She could be anywhere in the harbor or out on the Sound or up the Hudson. I would stay on for the weekend. Then it was back to the truck driving job on Monday.

It took about two months, but I finally got my union card and a job as a deckhand on the good towboat *Emily Jean.* I was off and running. We did a lot of oil barge work in the winter. When the sand and gravel slowed down, I started talking to the bargemen. It looked like a pretty good job. The work was steadier, and it paid a hell of a lot more money than working the deck of a tugboat. So I went down to the coast guard, got the literature I needed, studied hard, and sat for my tankerman's ticket. I passed the test and walked out a certified tankerman, grade b and lower, which includes all petroleum products up to and including gasoline. I went to work for Morania Oil Tanker Corp on the barge *Morania 180*, with Captain Joe Kapster. He lived in Poughkeepsie, NY, and he was known to one and all as Poughkeepsie Joe.

When I came aboard I was pretty green. I may have passed the test at the coast guard, but loading and pumping a real live barge was another story. She was what was called a canaler, not a big boat just 20,000 barrels. They were built to fit in the locks on the New York State barge canal system, which were 241 feet long and 43 feet wide. I worked on the 180 from February 1980 to April 1981. She was going into the yard for a major overhaul. I was transferred to a tanker. We called them self-propellers. She was the *Morania Abaco*, a small asphalt tanker. She delivered her loads at a temperature of 275 to 300 degrees. She was a traveler. We picked up and delivered loads all up and down the East Coast, up to Canada, and through the Great Lakes. The place that I liked best was Newfoundland. It was beautiful and had the nicest and most honest people I've ever met in all of my travels. The worst people? Quebec, specifically Montreal. Hands down the worst people to deal with. They can speak English but won't. They are just all-around shitheads. Toronto ranks right up there with the Newfies. They are a very pleasant people. Thankfully, most of our dealings with Canadian customs took place in Toronto. They came aboard, looked at our paperwork, had a cup of tea, and left us about our business. Quebec was the exact opposite. They practically stripped the crew. In fact, we had to bring stool samples with us when we flew into Montreal at crew change time. I assume that they were thrown out. It was just their way of letting us know that they didn't like an American crew sailing intra-Canadian.

We did a lot of fishing off of the *Abaco*. In fact, the company put a big freezer on board to keep our catch in, and we kept pretty near full all of the time. We used twenty-six–ounce jigs on hand lines. We would drift over a bank, where the water was only about two hundred feet deep, and pull them in one after the other. No sport here. This was mass production. The bottom must have been covered with them. Of course, there will always be somebody greedier than the next guy. We had the chief engineer, old Tommy Tonilan, beside the jig. He put a couple of hooks farther up the line. On a trip up to Seven Isles, up near Labrador, we stopped to fish. We were hauling them in big time. Tommy was using his gang hook line. He pulled in a huge cod of forty to fifty pounds. He laid it down and reached for his pliers to remove the hook. This fifty-pound cod rolled over the side and headed for the bottom. Tommy grabbed the line, which was now whizzing over the side. Here came one of those greed hooks right through Tommy's hand. He was hollering like a stuck pig. "Somebody, quick, cut the line to ease the pressure on his hand!" He passed out around that time, and the captain came down, looked at Tommy's hand, and told me to hold it steady. He pushed the hook all the way through, cut off the barb, and removed the hook. Then we took him to his room and put him to bed. The next day we arrived at Seven Isles. We tied up at the pier, hooked up our hoses, and started discharging. On the other side of the dock was a shell tanker with a Filipino crew. They were hauling in nice fat flounder, one after the other. Everybody off watch rigged up to fish. Here came Tommy, still hurting from yesterday. He rigged up his pole, baited it, and instead of just dropping his line like everybody else, he cast it out, where the big ones supposedly lurked. The hook caught his eyeglasses and they went over the side. Tommy went back to his cabin for the rest of the trip.

I worked for two captains on the *Abaco*, depending on the crew change overlap. John Botch was a pleasure to work with, and Phinias Smith was, for the lack of a better word, an asshole. He lived in a fantasy world. In his world, the *Abaco* was transformed from an old rust bucket that shuttled asphalt from port to port into a sleek Greyhound of the seas. Instead of ten knots, she whipped along in excess of thirty-five. In his world, he took his meals at the captain's table and dined with dignitaries. The fact was that we ate at a very long table in the galley. The original crew numbered twenty-five. We now sailed her with eight, so there were at most three or four men eating at a time. They would be at one end of the table, and old Smitty would be at the other end. His dignitary would probably be one of the pilots. We took two aboard for the transit of the St. Lawrence seaway, which took thirty-seven hours. Smitty would regale him with tales of adventure on the high seas while delivering hot asphalt. But pilot or no pilot, Smitty never dined with the troops. He preferred exile at his end of the table.

As luck would have it, I was usually on his watch, so I had the dubious pleasure of eating all three meals in his company. Breakfast was by far the best. He was a health nut. Every morning it was oatmeal, about thirty-seven pills, and anything in the condiment tray. At breakfast that would include salt, pepper, grape jelly, orange marmalade, honey, and cinnamon. He would add a little milk to his oatmeal and then all of the above, plus the thirty-seven pill mix down the hatch—a real breakfast of champions.

The crew on the *Abaco* were mostly Norwegians, a very stubborn—and I might add thick—people. They didn't call them squareheads for nothing. "Dot is nut der vay ve doo it" was all I heard. If you try to show them an easier way to do something, check the above.

There were exceptions. The cook was from Narvik. That's above the arctic circle. He was a great cook. He must have had a thousand different ways to cook cod. As I mentioned, we had a freezer full of it. He would steam the livers and put them in a bowl at my seat. I loved them. We once had codfish fritters for breakfast. They were yummy with a little maple syrup and butter.

When I first came aboard the *Abaco*, I was the dayman. I basically worked an eight-hour day, but I was on call whenever they needed an extra hand. It made for a lot of overtime, but if Smitty was on as captain, he would roust me out of my bunk at 6:00 AM, even if I flopped at five. John Botch as captain would let me sleep in.

Chris Rodal and Stanley Romano were the two watch ABs who I usually worked with. For the uninitiated, AB stands for "able-bodied" seaman, but we were always referred to as just ABs. Chris Rodal lived in Norway. He kept an apartment in Brooklyn, and he went home once a year for a month to see his wife and family. Stanley lived in the Greenpoint section of Brooklyn. He spent his life sailing throughout the Far East with American President Lines. The *Abaco* was his winding-down job before he retired for real. It was a pleasure to work with both of them.

Chris Rodal retired and went back to Norway, but I don't think retirement suited him. We heard that he took a job on a reefer ship hauling grapes from Portugal to Norway, but I moved into his watch AB job. We got a new dayman aboard, and he was—you guessed it—Norwegian. His name was Gunnar Tieland. I'll tell you about him later.

I will give you two examples of what it was like sailing with Norwegians. One was the seating arrangement at the galley table. I mentioned before that the *Abaco* had accommodations for a crew of twenty-five. There were two dining tables in the galley. One was for officers and one was for the crewmen. The officers' table was used for board games and cards. No one ate at that table. Everyone ate at the crew's table. There was room for fourteen diners at that table, and as I mentioned before, only four of us ate at a time. When I was the dayman, I sat at the end of the table, which was fine with me. Being left-handed, I didn't have to worry about poking anybody with my elbow. When Chris Rodal retired, I moved into his job as watch AB. I didn't realize I would also have to shift over one seat to the right, into the seat formerly occupied by Chris. All seats in the galley were assigned according to your position on board. This left nine empty seats. Gunnar and I agreed not to change seats, since he was right-handed and I was left-handed. I would stay in the end seat. It wasn't to be. When the chief came in and sat down to eat, he was horrified to look up and see me sitting across from him in my old seat. He first complained to the cook, and then he started yelling in Norwegian at Gunnar about disrupting the status quo and me being a troublemaker. I don't think the chief was one of my biggest fans. But we had to swap seats to keep peace, I was told.

The first time I met Gunnar was at the airport in Toronto, Canada. He was coming aboard for the first time. The night before I received two phone calls. One was from Bill Overiemer, the port captain, advising me that we were getting a new crew member by the name of Gunnar Tieland and to watch out for him at the airport and see that he gets to the boat okay. "No problem," I said. A little while later I got another phone call, this time from Gunnar's wife. Gunnar had sailed the Great Lakes for many years, and he had a drinking problem at one time. She wanted to know if I or any of the crew on the *Abaco* had a problem. "Not as far as I know." We all had a drink now and then, but we always came up the gangway under our own steam. Then she wanted to talk to Judy. Obviously, Gunnar was a real pip, and she didn't trust him as far as she could throw him. She had him nailed.

The next morning I arrived at the airport and checked in for my flight. I asked the clerk if a Gunnar Tieland had checked in yet. He was already on board in seat 54a. Good, I wouldn't have to look for him. I boarded the plane and looked for his seat to introduce myself. I got to seat 54a and found this very inebriated passenger dribbling all over his shirtfront and mumbling to himself. I kept right on going to my own seat. I would catch Gunnar later. He slept during the flight, and his head kept falling onto the shoulder of the poor guy next to him. Every time the stewardess walked past his seat, she would carefully check out the overhead storage. They didn't want to know anything.

When we were safely off the plane and on the concourse, I introduced myself to him. "Gunnar, my name is Bob Vargovcik, I'm an A.B. on the *Abaco*. We'll share a cab to the boat." His reply? "I need a drink." My reply? "You're out of luck. Bars in Canada don't open until noon." It was now ten o'clock. He broke out into an instant cold sweat. It was literally pouring down his forehead in a torrent. I thought he was going into shock. Anyway, we got aboard and settled in for the next couple of <u>weeks</u>.

The next time we changed crews in Toronto, Gunnar was ready. His carry-on bag was full of booze. I counted eight bottles. It took him three days to finish them off—three days spent curled up on his bunk alternately sucking on his thumb or a bottle of booze. Smitty was captain, and he never said a word. He liked Gunnar. Gunnar used to throw all that "Yes, sir!" and "Aye-aye" shit at him, and Smitty ate it up.

Gunnar ended up being a battle casualty. We had a coil of poly-pro mooring line aboard. I don't know who ordered it, but we had six hundred feet of it lying in the foc"sul. It was dangerous line to work with. Mooring line under pressure gets very hot. The first line out is the spring line, which is used to position the ship at the dock. Tying up puts a tremendous amount of strain on this line: the engines are pushing the ship forward while the seaman on the line holds her back, controlling its forward motion by easing it out until the mate on watch signals that the ship is in position.

The trouble with plastic line is that it gets so hot being served around a bit that it melts and sticks to the bit. Eventually, the power of the ship's engines will cause it to break loose—and woe to the seaman who is serving that line! You can't let go of it fast enough.

Now, Gunnar, having been around long enough to know better—but perhaps his judgment was clouded by booze—was on the line. Smitty told him to break out that nice new poly-pro. "Aye-aye, sir," barked Gunnar.

We were alongside the dock, ahead slow. All of a sudden, there was a loud report, not unlike a large-caliber gun shot, and Gunnar went flying up the deck, ass over teakettle. When he landed, we could see his right arm was about two feet longer than his left.

They took him off to the hospital to reset his severely dislocated shoulder. Needless to say, we never saw Gunnar again.

I've also mentioned John Botch. He was the other captain, and a pleasure to work with. Besides being an AB., I was also a certified tanker man, which meant that I could stand deck watch during a cargo transfer unsupervised, whereas the other ABs had to have a licensed officer on deck with them. Captain Botch loved it when I took over the watch job after Chris Rodal's retirement. Whenever we were dockside doing a cargo transfer, one of us could sleep in while the other covered the deck watch.

John loved cigars. He couldn't smoke at home; he had an asthmatic daughter who had to have oxygen available for her attacks. If the oxygen didn't explode, the smoke would have killed her. So when he was on board the *Abaco*, he smoked with a vengeance—humidors full, I think.

Eddie Wilson was the assistant engineer. He retired from the coast guard after twenty-seven years of service, most of which he spent driving a pickup truck with a thirteen-foot Boston whaler behind it. His job was maintaining aids to navigation located on riverbanks, but he got his sea time whenever he launched the whaler. How he got his license, we never found out, but hey, at least he had one. Eddie's dreams of a relaxing retirement were short-lived. He didn't even get to put his La-Z-Boy into the reclined position before his wife handed him a bucket and soggy rag and set him to cleaning this wall and that floor and those windows. He figured the only way he would get any rest and relaxation was to go back to work. Being a licensed engineer, it was fairly easy to get a union card, and so when Morania called the union hall for an engineer, they sent Eddie.

Now, Eddie wasn't really an engineer; he just had a piece of paper. Think about it; if you had worked twenty-seven years for the bank or down at the plant, they'd probably give you a gold watch or maybe a gold pen and pencil set for all of years of faithful service when you retried. The coast guard gave Eddie an engineer's license, probably assuming he'd never actually use it. They didn't know Eddie. He figured, *Hey, I have an engineer's license, so I must be one.* He never lacked for confidence, despite the fact that he got lost on his way to the engine room. Although the *Abaco was diesel powered*, she had a boiler that supplied steam to the coils in the cargo tanks to keep the product hot. Eddie thought that it was a pretty small boiler to power a ship the size of the *Abaco.* Eddie was a licensed engineer for motor ships that is diesel powered ships. To say that the office was dismayed at his observation would be an understatement, but the ship couldn't sail without two licensed engineers. We cast off all lines and off we went.

One more Eddie story. Eddie and I were both off watch, just relaxing in the galley, when in comes Stanley Romano, my partner. He was on watch, getting coffee for the wheelhouse. He was rubbing his neck; he said it was bothering him, probably a stiff neck from sitting in a draught. We were on our way to Nova Scotia, and had just passed through the East River into Long Island Sound. I told him his problem came from craning his neck trying to look into those penthouse windows facing the river. We always checked out these windows—you never knew what you would see. The people living there thought that they had all of this privacy.

"No,"—he looks at me and winks—"I think it's from the dog collar."

Eddie looks at him and asks, "The dog collar? What dog collar?"

Stanley is in the process of filling the coffee mugs. "The one my wife makes me wear when I'm home," says Stanley, from over where he's filling the mugs.

Eddie sits there, stunned. Finally he whispers, "She makes you wear a dog collar?"

"Yep!" Stanley tells him happily. "And a leash. She also got this little whip. If I'm bad she whips me with it. Even if I'm good she'll give me a couple of licks for good measure." With that as a parting shot, Stanley goes back up to the wheelhouse with the coffees, leaving me to finish the story. He knew he had Eddie hooked, and oh boy did he. Eddie was all over me with questions, so I told all about the scars on Stanley's back, which was why he always wore a shirt. I said he got the idea out of the *Penthouse* forum to spice up their sex life, but it got out of hand, and Stanley didn't know how to stop it.

"She's even buying leather clothes for them to wear, so you can feel the pain without the scars," I finished knowingly.

When I relieved Stanley at midnight, I filled him in on what I had added to the story. Eddie pestered Stanley for the rest of the trip for more details; he also kept trying to catch Stanley with his shirt off. He told Stanley that he read about that stuff all off the time in those magazines, but he didn't think anybody actually did it. Stanley told him that he ought to give it a try. He might like it. Eddie never mentioned it … but we'll never know.

Jan Hogan was the cook, and a very good one. He never

sat down to eat a meal, just ate all three standing up in the galley while he cooked. He sampled everything as he went along. We would go up the street together for a couple of beers, and I usually went grub shopping with him. One time we sat down in this small bar to have a quiet beer when a motorcycle gang roared in. I mean right *into* the place. They parked their bikes right next to their tables. They were all decked out in their finest leather: the girls had on leather pants and bikini tops. The temperature was in the 90s. I guess they were trying to keep cool. Anyway, Jan and I beat a hasty retreat.

Tom Phelps was the other cook. I also went food shopping with him. Tom liked to take a taste now and then. When you're buying a thousand bucks of grub at a time, the store manager treats you right. To Tommy that meant a bottle in the back room of the store while yours truly did the shopping. I usually had to carry the groceries back to the boat. I also had to tote our inebriated cook back on board, though I must say that no matter how drunk Tommy was, he always put out a good meal.

Ray Spitzer was another AB. He was on the other crew. He kept two military uniforms in his locker, one army, one navy. He was either an army major or a naval lieutenant commander. He figured that since we usually were tied up near some kind of military base, he could sit there and drink good booze at cheap prices (if he paid at all). He claimed most of the time he just signed a chit, and he knew enough about the military to bullshit his way through. He never got caught, as far as I know.

Then there was Kenny Olafson, relieving chief engineer, he was dying of stomach cancer but he didn't want to stay at home and die. The way he had it figured he would be a much bigger pain in the ass to everybody if he kicked the bucket on board. We wholeheartedly agreed, he was a pain in the ass already, and he wasn't dead yet. We told him we would just stuff him in the freezer with the cod and keep him in there until we got back to New York, then dump him on the dock and let the office worry about it. Kenny died not long after I left the *Abaco*. He didn't check out on board like he had hoped, but he still managed to be pain in the ass, at least to his girlfriend of thirty-six years. His body wasn't cold yet when his two sisters flew in from Norway, scooped up all of his money (which I understand was considerable), and flew home. He never made any provisions for his girlfriend, and the sisters screwed her royally.

Then there was John Delarenus, the mate, a very nice guy and a good seaman, but like Mel Tillis in reverse. He was fine holding a normal conversation, but when he had to talk on the VHF radio, he was a mess. As soon as he put that microphone in front of his face, he froze. He would start blabbering and stuttering so badly that he had to have an interpreter on watch with him. A few months after I met him, we were both working at Hess. I was on the barge ST114, and John was captain on a tanker, *the A. H. Dumont*. He was backing out of a slip in Brooklyn, and when he went from all stop to slow ahead, he lost power. No power, no steerage. The *Dumont* hit the dock dead on and stove in the bow. How I wish I had a tape recorder! For one thing, you don't put an "Oh, shit!" out over the air, but John's imitation of Porky Pig was priceless. It took him all of ten minutes to tell dispatch that he lost power and hit the dock. Of course, the coast guard monitors working channels for just what John just blurted out. They were all over John and the *Dumont* like bees on honey. That's what got John in trouble, not hitting the dock. When you lose power in a maneuvering situation, you grab a roll of toilet paper and clean underwear and cross your fingers, because there isn't much you can do at that point except drop the anchor. And in a close situation like John's, even that wouldn't have saved him. Still, because he cussed on the airwaves, the company gave him such a hard time that he up and retired.

My career on the *Abaco* ended up in Newfoundland—Stevensville, to be exact. I was due to get off, and Judy and I had reservations to get away for a couple of days in Cape May, New Jersey. Admiral Smith told me that I had to wait six more days to get relieved. When we arrived back in Montreal, he explained that it was too expensive to get a flight from Newfoundland to Montreal, and then one to New York. I called Morania, and they had no problem with the Newfoundland flight, so I called my relief and made the arrangement. There was only one flight a day; the plane spends twenty minutes on the ground and then leaves. Smitty advised me to wait on board for my relief to show up, which was normal, but in this case, I wanted to spend a very expensive night ashore. Another phone call to the office, and they told me that I could meet the plane. If my man wasn't on it, I would return to the boat. Fair enough.

When I walked down the gangway with my sea bag, Smitty said that I would be fired as soon as I stepped ashore. I told him where to go and how to get there, and off I went. Luckily my man was on the plane. We shook hands, which made his relieving me official, and thus ended my career on board the *Abaco*.

Judy and I went on our mini-vacation. When we returned, I called the union looking for another job. I was offered an AB job on the tanker *A. H. Dumont, which would later have the encounter with the Brooklyn pier, under the command of Captain John Delarenus a job that* I immediately turned down. The union called me back with another job sailing as mate on board the barge ST 114, owned by Spentonbush Redstar Towing, which was actually Hess Oil. She was loaded and ready to sail. I had to be at Port Reading as soon as possible. I grabbed my sea bag, and off I went.

Well, talk about from the frying pan into the fire: I traded an egomaniac for a boozer. This man would drink a case of beer in one sitting, I kid you not. He was also uncomfortable with physical labor in any way shape or form. Many times he would go up the street, supposedly to buy groceries, and not come back to stand his watch, sticking me with it. I made two trips with him, and then I gave the company the mandatory three days' notice.

I quit the boat in Albany, N.Y., and by the time I got home, the company had called and asked if I would return to work on the opposite watch. I agreed and returned to the ST 114 to work with a redneck by the name of Ricky Strong. He was a good old boy from Florida. He knew somebody in the office, so he'd gotten hired as barge captain, but he didn't know his ass from a hole in the ground when it came to barges. He just had a mate's license for a tug. However, thanks to the license, he didn't need a tankerman's ticket, the lucky SOB. He lasted a couple of trips and walked off with no notice, just disappeared. The tug captain wouldn't sail with the barge shorthanded, so we tied up and waited for a replacement.

The Office sends an A.B.off a tanker to take over the captain's job and this time I rebelled. This guy didn't know anything about barges either! He had just come off of a tanker. I called the union; they advised me not to let him aboard, since his appointment didn't come through the union. The company threatened to fire me, but when I told them what the union had said, they backed down. At two that morning, I found myself facing the kid's replacement from the union hall. Finally, we sailed.

When we arrived at our destination, I was told to call the office on a land line. *Uh-oh!* I thought. But I wasn't fired;

instead, they offered me the captain's job. Not that they liked me, but they knew that they wouldn't get any hassle from the union. And thus began my seven-year career with Hess Oil.

I enjoyed the job, and I loved the boat. She was big, 420 feet long and sixty-eight feet wide, and she drew twenty-eight feet fully loaded. It came to an abrupt halt on February 15, 1988. That was when we were locked out and replaced by coon-assed scabs from Louisiana. The great strike of 1988, Hess sent me a letter advising me that if I did not resign my membership in the union, I would be terminated. Personally, I never could or would leave the union; I'd been a union man all my life and would remain so for the next two years. I did picket duty at first on a regular basis, but it tapered off gradually. I would go when I received a call, usually to picket a stockholder's meeting or some other event. But in the meantime, I had to get a job.

*My sister and i in front of one of my mothers
gigantic christmas trees, 1943*

*My cousin maryjane on my right, my sister on my left, posing on our boat in Union Beach, N.J.*

*Here i am ten years old ,an altar boy at St.Joseph's church.*

*autumn 1956, my parents, my sister in her nun uniform, me in my army uniform.*

*This picture was taken in 1958 on the greenland ice cap, i was a 21 year old army specialist, note the scenery in the background.*

*M. T./Morania Abaco, discharging in Stevenville Newfoundland, 1981.*

*My Cookn' Good truck.*

*Taken at our 40th.wedding anniversary party,my beautiful wife,and three great children,Kris,Rob, and Nancy.*

*My wife and I on vacation in Las Vegas.*

*This is the boat that i built on launching day.*

# CHAPTER 10: THE BIG STRIKE OF 88, A GAME CHANGER

I went to work for Yellow Freight out of their Elizabeth terminal. I pulled double trailers either to Cleveland or Buffalo. I liked it; the money and benefits were very good, although the hours were a little hectic. All the loads were dispatched, off what they called the wheel,there was no actual wheel,but when your name came up,no matter what time of the day it was,you got a call ,you picked your load according to seniority if there was more than one load, and headed out. The worst time was winter. Crossing those Pennsylvania mountains during a snowstorm was no picnic. We used to joke about the mechanics having to pry our fingers off the steering wheel when we arrived at our destination, but it wasn't too far from the truth.

In 1990 the union called me with a job: mate on the *Richmond*, a barge owned by Reinauer Transportation in Staten Island, New York the captain was a Yugoslav guy named Stanley Ruskin. He was a pretty good skate, and we got along fine. The *Richmond* was a small 43,000-barrel barge, and we ran mixed loads of gasoline between New York and Rocky Hill, Connecticut, for Citgo Oil. I started work on the Richmond in February. In May, Stanley was hurt pretty seriously when he was knocked over the side by swinging cargo hose. Unfortunately, instead of landing in the water, he landed on the dock. He never did return to work, and I was again promoted to captain. That lasted until September, when the mate working with me opened the wrong valves and contaminated 9,000 barrels of high-test gasoline. In the space of a week, Judy and I arrived at our new home in Maryland, and I was fired.

I'd never been fired in my life, and the incident sparking it wasn't even my fault. I would have felt a little better if it had been my fault, because at least then I'd have done the screwing up. This was just perverse; they didn't even have the guts to fire me face-to-face. When I was sitting across the desk from the port captain, I told him, "If you're going to fire me, do it now. I'll clear all off my gear off of the boat and I'll be out of here."

"No, no, it won't come to that," he hurried to assure me. "We'll just put a letter in your file, and that'll be the end of it."

So I went home, driving from Staten Island all the way back to Ocean City, Maryland. The next morning the phone rang. Judy picked it up; her eyes widened, and she said, "Okay, I'll tell him."

"Who was that?" I asked her.

"You've just been fired," she said.

I tried to call old Joe back, but he wasn't available.

Judy and I stayed unemployed for a month. We just bopped around the area, getting the lay of the land. Then I got a job with Cookin' Good Chicken, hauling processed chicken up and down the east coast, and Judy went to work at the Sears store in Salisbury, selling water heaters and water softeners. We still chuckle about that. She didn't know one from the other, and there she was telling customers how much better the Sears product was over the competition. Talk about the blind leading the blind.

I'd been with Cookin' Good about four months when I got a call about a boat job. The port captain at Morania Oil called the union and asked if I was available for a new barge they had just bought from Texaco. They wanted me for the captain job. I was flattered; that was also a first for me, having a company call the union specifically asking for me. I accepted it immediately. The only catch was that it meant being away a month at a time and only two weeks home in between. I still jumped on it.

I boarded the boat in Marcus Hook, Pennsylvania, at the Sunoco Refinery, as she was loading for New York. Morania had bought both the tug and the barge ,at 1600—that's 4:00 P.M. to you landlubbers, The tug captain and I both went aboard, and we signed for both vessels. The painters came aboard and painted over the Texaco names; then they stenciled in *Morania 5* on the tug and *Morania 460* on the barge. She was big: 460 feet long, 84 feet wide, drawing 34 feet loaded. The number 460, funny enough, had nothing to do with her length; Morania named their barges in sequence. The previous barge was the 450, and before that was the 440, and so on. The *460* had a capacity of 180,000 barrels, but 30,000 of that was ballast, so her real payload topped out at 150,000 barrels. She also had a boiler to keep the cargo hot. Captaining her was a big responsibility, but I loved it, and I was glad to be back on the water. The downside was that I had to work with the scabs. The union couldn't get qualified replacements for them, so they had to stay on the barge. I had one scab out of three men, and he was a pretty good kid—Scotty Thornfell from Mississippi. The tug was about half and half, union and scab. At first there were a lot of hard feelings, but gradually everyone let bygones be bygones, and we pretty much got along.

I worked with two tug captains during that job. Kim Dubouis hailed from Louisiana. He was a good boatman, and easy to get along with—plus, he was a great cook. He made this fantastic Cajun food, and many a time he sent us over an incredible meal. We'd reciprocate with fresh-baked donuts or molasses corn muffins. One year, we arrived at our discharge point, Providence, Rhode Island, on Christmas morning. I would be busy all day discharging cargo, which meant no time to cook a Christmas dinner. Kim came alongside and sent up dinners for both of us.

The other captain, was a different story altogether. Leaving aside the fact that he was redneck from the Florida panhandle, and a lousy boatman, he was also a crybaby. He ran to the office for everything. He can best be summed in one word: asshole. I once got into an argument with him over some of his petty bullshit. I told him that I refused to get into a battle of wits with an unarmed man. He just looked at me. He knew that what I just said wasn't good, but he didn't know what the hell I said, so he asked the mate. Marvin told him that I wasn't exactly patting him on the back and let it go at that. Old Marvin stayed out of politics; maybe that's normal when you're from Mobile, though. I don't really know too many guys from Alabama.

We ran up and down the east coast with the *460* busy all of the time. We also went from four weeks on and two weeks off, to three and three. It cut my pay a little, but I liked the extra time off. So did Judy.

After a while, though, even just three weeks on got to be a long three weeks. Plus, I had a relief who wanted my job. Didn't matter that we already made the same money; I was the senior captain, and he wanted that title. He was constantly trying to set me up. On crew-change day, my mate and I would go over the boat with a fine-toothed comb. We were always finding something: an open valve that should be closed, a closed valve that should be open, and so on. I eventually got tired of the cat-and-mouse games, and the office was no help, so I quit and went back to the trucks.

I got my job back with Cookin' Good and kept it for two years. The road isn't the water, though, so finally I caved and called the union up. "You have to have a job for me," I said. They did. In May of '95, I went back, and was I ever glad to be there. I was now captain of the good ship *Janet C.*, a 55,000 barrel barge. Poling Transportation up in Staten Island owner her. She was a piece of junk, but I didn't care as long as she stayed afloat..

I was on the *Janet* about four months when she was sold to, of all companies, Reinauer. They asked to come over with the barge. I explained the fact that I was fired five years ago for being incompetent; did they really want me back now? They explained that they'd realized it was my mate who made the mistake, not me.

"Well," I said, "how 'bout back pay and lost seniority?"

They explained that they weren't that sorry.

I eventually got my seniority back because it didn't cost them anything, and that and a buck would get me on the subway. Reinauer was a very cheap company; when they bought the *Janet C.*, they also purchased the *Robert L. Poling*, a 70,000 barrel boat just a little bigger than the *Janet*. They renamed the *Janet* the *RTC 55*, and the *Robert L.* became the *RTC 70*. They offered me the captains job on the 70 and I jumped at it. She was big enough to be a steady working boat, but not big enough to work you to death. She was a bit of an ugly duckling, but I got really attached to her. She would be my last boat; at fifty-eight, I had only four years left to work.

One guy, my opposite when I was a captain (meaning he was on the other watch) was a fellow named Steve Ralstan. When he flew up from Florida, on crew change day, he took to visiting relatives, then doing his grub shopping. He was a terrible relief. I had a Ford pickup that I parked at Reinauer's yard at Erie Basin in Brooklyn. On crew change day, Steve and his mate Tony Flucker, who lived in Savannah, would fly into New York, , meet at Erie Basin, and drive my truck to wherever the boat was. Ralston was so cheap, he estimated that my truck got about thirty miles per gallon, so if he drove ninety miles to the boat, he would put three gallons of gas in. But the company was giving him twenty-eight cents per mile for travel money! Tony finally shamed him into filling the tank. He clued him into the fact that I paid for the truck, the insurance, and the maintenance.

Tony was a wiz of a bargeman. There wasn't anything he couldn't do on a barge. The only thing keeping him from a captain's job was John Barleycorn. Tony liked his booze, but when he did stop drinking, he moved right into a captain's job. Tony was a real redneck. He lived in a trailer park and had a girlfriend who drove him around in his own truck when he was home on his time off—his license was gone forever after his third DUI. Tony also didn't have a phone. If you had to get in touch with him on his time off, you called his mother, and she would track him down. When he left to go back to the boat for two weeks, his neighbors would get into his trailer, drink all his beer, eat all his food, watch his TV, and borrow his VCR. You can just imagine what his phone bill would be with neighbors like that. I'll give an idea: his last bill, before he got rid of the phone, was a hair under a thousand, and he was only home two weeks.

When Carlos Ramos came aboard, things changed. The guy was just a bit weird. He did not have much of a social life. I mean, come on—he was thirty-six years old and lived with his mother. He spent a lot of his off time working on other boats; he thought he was in solid with the office because of all of the extra time he put in on these other boats. And he was … to a point. We worked together for two and a half years, during which time we got along pretty well. But alas, it was not to last. We were one day out of the shipyard, and I was getting ready for our first load, kerosene from Shell in Seawaren, New Jersey. I told Carlos to put down his video game and secure some manhole covers that had been removed for inspection while we were in dry dock. He blew up, threatened me, and tried to throw me overboard. Well, that was the end of our working together. I told him that his days on the *70* were over. He laughed and told me that he was Reinauer's golden boy and that I would be the one taken off the boat. The office had a tug stand by to make sure that I didn't go over the side before the barge superintendent arrived. Carlos was a big boy, and I didn't want to mess with him. And, of course, Carlos was told to pack his bags.

After Carlos, I got a mate by the name of Mick Latrel. He hailed from Pensacola, Florida.. He was a good barge mate, easygoing and knew his stuff. But he had a hell of a personal life! One thing about working on a barge: there are just two of you, so you spend as much time with your crewmate as you do with your wife—sometimes more. There aren't very many things that aren't touched on during your couple of weeks together. I had thirty-plus years on Mick (in fact, I was older than his father) so he told me his problems: how he was married and divorced from a wife that he was not particularly fond of, to put it mildly; how he had a little boy he adored. He was now living with a woman ten years older than he was, and she wanted to get married, but Mick was understandably reluctant. He had come to the conclusion that all women were either sluts or bitches. I tried to convince him otherwise. On my next-to-last trip, Mick left the company to go work over at Bouchard Transportation. His father worked there, and he was going to work the same cycle so they could drive up from Florida together and save money. Also, Mick was scared of flying, and the only direct flight that he could get out of Pensacola to New York was on Valu-Jet, which had had a very bad crash in the Everglades. They changed their name to try to foster a new image, but they couldn't fool Mick. Anyway, he said he was going to try the marriage bit again, and he planned on moving over the line to Alabama. I liked Mick, and I wished him well, though I wished he could have stayed one more trip so I wouldn't have to break a new mate in. With this job, you meet a lot of good people, and then they move to different boats and you often don't see them again. Of course with some people it worked out great—you never wanted to see them again anyway.

When I worked over at Poling, my mate at the time was a fellow by the name of Jimmy Calamar. I had known Jimmy for about twenty years; we sailed on different boats, but we were running the New York barge canal system for Morania tankers, and we ran into each other quite a bit. We were both sailing as mates when we met, I was on the *Morania 180*, and Jimmy was on the *160*. *His* captain drove Jimmy nuts he had a young wife from Columbia, a real knockout; they lived in a condo with a pool, right in Staten Island. He was a wreck from worrying about her lounging around the pool in her bikini, making eyes at all of her fellow tenants; in fact, he was getting so upset over it that he moved them to Florida. I didn't get it; instead of shaking her butt around the pool for three or four months of the year, she had twelve months to let it all hang out! Needless to say, they were soon on their way to splitsville.

Not long after that Jimmy showed up as a mate on the Hess barge *Hygrade 42*. Morania had started scrapping some of the older barges, and Jimmy had to move on. We both stayed at Hess until the strike in 1988. When I went to work driving over the road for Yellow freight, Jimmy went to work driving a Yellow Cab. When I went back to work for Poling, I didn't know that they were broke; during the strike, the daughter and son-in-law bled the company dry. sometimes it was a long stretch between pay checks, As I'm sitting at the Northville Petroleum Dock in Linden, waiting for a mate for my piece-of-shit boat to show up, a cab pulls up to the end of the dock, and who should step out but Jimmy! He climbed up the ladder from the dock, got on his knees, and kissed the deck. Then he put his arms around me and picked me straight up off the deck. Thankfully he didn't kiss me. I told him he was like a bad penny I couldn't get rid of. But still, I was glad to see him. Jimmy had a bit of a past; he was what New Yorkers call "connected," meaning he had ties to the mob. On his off time, Jimmy was an enforcer for the loan sharks—he liked to say that if you owed money to said loan shark and were a little behind on your payments, Jimmy would encourage you to catch up.

That was in fact his undoing; he was caught on tape, and he got four years for it. He came back to the boat one time with two new pairs of sneakers. "Whats' the deal with new shoes I asked.

"For when I do my time," he replied. "The sneakers that they give you when you go to jail are garbage." I nodded in agreement—as if I knew.

Jimmy was old school; he believed in *omerta*, sealed lips. I told him all the other guys involved were singing like canaries and they weren't going to jail. "But you're keeping your mouth shut, and looking at four years," I added. He didn't care what they did; he'd do his own thing. One time we were chugging up Newark Bay with a load of gas bound for the Texaco terminal in Newark, and a state marine police boat pulled up alongside. Two FBI agents came aboard, put the cuffs on Jimmy, and told him he was going ashore for questioning

Jimmy piped up, saying, "I need a life jacket! If I fall overboard with these cuffs on, I'll drown like a rat." So they uncuffed him, asked me for a life jacket, put it on him, recuffed him, and hauled him off. He came back three days later ... minus the life jacket.

Jimmy was a hell of a nice guy, but he had two sides. I dealt with the nice side. Once he told me to stay home a couple of extra days, because I was due to come back to work the day before Thanksgiving. I was able to enjoy the day at home thanks to him. Then there was his other side, the one that, I think, could probably take you apart piece by piece. Jimmy lost his merchant marine document because of his conviction. I guess if I want to see him again, I'll have to go back to Bayonne and call a cab.

After the strike, a lot of the Yugos who had worked for Poling moved to Reinauer, but at least there they spoke English. The captain I'd worked with, Stanley, wasn't a bad guy. We were on charter to Citgo Oil, running gas from the Arthur Kill River mostly to Rocky Hill, Connecticut. It wasn't bad work, but on one memorable trip, loading at Exxon in Linden, Stanley was hit by a cargo hose. I was asleep at the time, and the dockman came aboard and woke me up. I went up on deck, took one look, and oh boy—I knew right away that he was in bad shape.

Now Stanley was no tough guy, didn't tolerate a lot of pain. A few weeks prior, in fact, Stanley was on deck chipping some rust without goggles. "Stanley," I said, "put on a pair of goggles before you get something in your eye."

"Nah; I'm going to just finish this little bit, Bobby." Almost before the words were out, a little speck flew up. He screamed bloody murder. "Oh shit! Shit, Bobby, I just got something in my eye!" He was hysterical. I took a look; his eye was all bloodshot and teary when we got to the dock ,I called a cab and sent him to the emergency room. He came back with a big eye patch and some eye drops. He was supposed to put the drops in his eyes three times a day, but he couldn't do it; every time he put the dropper near his eye, it would close. He moaned, "Bobby, I cannot do this! My eye won't stay open." I ended up straddling his chest, forcing his eye open, and squeezing the drops in.

Now here he was looking like the last rose of summer, white as a sheet, trying to support his arm, which was obviously giving him a lot of pain. He looked at me and said, "Bobby, I think I did it this time.."

"Don't worry; they'll fix you up like new," I assured him. They took Stanley away in an ambulance. Well, he was right, he really had done it that time: he never came back to work because of the damage to his neck and shoulder. He wrecked them so bad he could no longer lift up his left arm. He sued Exxon and Reinauer both, but I don't think he made out, even though I testified on his behalf.

*I took over as captain on the Richmond.* I figured that it would be temporary; at that point we didn't know that Stanley wouldn't be coming back. They gave me a mate by the name of Richie Graham. I remember thinking, *Seven years here and he's still a mate?* I knew his father, a captain over at Morania, a very nice guy. Too bad his son was a flake. The day he came aboard, he put his sea bag down on the deck and showed me his profile. "Check me out! Who do I look like?" he asked.

I told him, how the hell do I know ,who do you want me to say that you look like.

He shook his head. "No, man, look again." I said nothing, so he went on, "Sly Stallone!"

Inwardly I rolled my eyes; there was absolutely no resemblance, but what the hell, I'd humor him and call him "Sly." Later the boy came out on deck to go on watch all decked out in tailored work clothes—I mean, they looked like were painted on.

Around this time the movie *Moonstruck*, starring Cher and Nicholas Cage, was in theaters. In the movie, Cage worked in a bakery. Richie figured that was the job that got you the babes. He quit the boats and got a job in a bakery. Of course, then he found out that the hours were shitty and the work was hard—hell, those flour sacks weigh about a hundred pounds each. One night of dumping flour into mixing machines and he was back looking for his job. I was the unlucky one, though, because he was one bad news bear: he eventually messed up a load of gas and got me fired. Karma paid him back not too long after I was gone, when he failed a drug screen test, and then he was also history.

Later on the *460*, I was again working with the best mate I ever worked with, Scotty Hampton. The Hamptons were Tories during the revolutionary war. They stuck with the king—bad move. They ended up moving up to Nova Scotia, where they founded the town of Hampton, which still exists today. Scotty showed it to me on a map. After the war they came back and all was forgiven; the house that Scotty lives in today, in Connecticut, has been in his family since the 1600s.

Scotty and I worked together for the first time in the summer of '82, on the Hess Barge *ST 114*. I was tied up in Baltimore when he came aboard. He was a very good mate. When he was on watch, you could sleep with both of your eyes closed. After I became a captain, he was the first mate I worked with, and he spoiled me, because I would never work with a mate as good as he was. We were together for two years when he was bumped by a senior man. He didn't want to leave, and I didn't want him to, but it eventually worked to his advantage: he was made captain on the barge *Ethel H.* But I missed him.

Scotty's replacement was a fellow by the name of Roy Turner who lived right around the corner from me in Bricktown. Again, he was a good bargeman, but he was a bit of an enigma. He usually didn't talk too much, but when he did he'd go on and on. One time we were changing crews at Bayonne, and Ray happened to have his truck parked there so he offered me a ride home. All I had left to do was sign the relieving report, which I told him.

"Well, hurry up; I'm leaving now," he said. I signed the report, which took all of about ten seconds, but when I got down to the end of the dock he was gone. That was Roy.

When the boat was working, I usually did all of the cooking and shopping. I guess I did all right; they all ate without complaining. One thing Roy never did was pay a compliment—he would just eat and grunt. When I retired, we were both working at Reinauer. On my last trip we were both tied up in Brooklyn waiting on orders, and Ray came over to visit, which wasn't usual for him. "I hear that you're retiring."

"Yep," I said.

"Would you give me the recipe for your pot roast?"

I was surprised and flattered at the same time. What really surprised me was the fact that we hadn't worked together for fourteen years and he still wanted the recipe. That must have been some pot roast.

'85, Roy left the *114*. He was going aboard the barge *Hygrade 22* to take over for a retiring captain. So on Christmas Day that year … well, I must have been a bad boy; I didn't get coal in my stocking, but I did get a new mate by the name Jimmy Moran. I was tied up in Bayonne and heard such a clatter that I looked over the side to see what the matter was. And what to my wondering eyes should appear but Jimmy Moran climbing the ladder with a big bag on his shoulder. But there were no toys in it. Jimmy was staying for a while.

Jimmy was previously mate on a barge where he gave the captain, John Murray, fits. He supposedly contaminated a couple of loads of gas by opening the wrong valve. So they sent him over to me. Merry Christmas! He started out like gangbusters, asking a lot of questions and putting notes in this little book that he carried. Very impressive—except that that was the first and last time I would see that particular book, or hear any of the questions that I answered for him. Still, Jimmy might not have been the sharpest knife in the drawer, but he was a genuinely nice guy. We would be together for a little over two years until the big strike of 1988, and we had a lot of fun and good times.

Jimmy was a big boy with an appetite to match. On several occasions, we would to ride the tug on coastwise trips. If the barge was loaded below her manned marks—I'm talking about the plimsoll mark on the side of all ships that tells you how deep you can load for different weather conditions, and different seasons and oceans—the crew was supposed to sail with the tug. Most tug captains let us stay on the barge. They knew that we preferred that, and two extra men on a tug made for tight living conditions. Anyway, whenever we had the tug *Atlantic Star*, we knew we would be on the tug. Jimmy was a big boy with an appetite to match; we called him Baby Huey. When we came aboard the *Star*, the first thing the cook did was lock up the refrigerator to keep Jimmy out. On a barge the captain and mate get an allowance of thirteen dollars a day for each man, but on a tug, the captain received ten bucks a day for each man. So whenever we rode the tug, I made sure that I paid the going rate for tug fare. In fact, I broke it down to $3.33 a meal. It used to piss them off. Technically I was in the right, but it was dirty pool, and I only did it with that one particular crew.

On one particular trip to Maine, Searsport to be exact, Jimmy slipped and fell on deck. He was limping a little; I told him to go back to the galley and get off his feet for a while. On the way home to New York, he was complaining about his knee. So when we docked at Bayonne, I sent him up to the hospital. The doctor who checked him out told him that he might need an operation but should get a second opinion. I got a call from dispatch; it seems that Jimmy called the office and was asking them if they thought he should get his knee operated on. I explained what the doctor meant by getting a second opinion and sent him home.

*Back on board the S.T.114,.* We had just finished lightering a ship at Stapleton anchorage and were under way to our discharge point. We still had our big three-thousand-pound fenders over the side; air motors raise and lower them. We were out there in the pitch dark, working by feel. I'm on one motor and Jimmy is on the other. Just as we start to raise the fender, Jimmy lets out a howl. It seems he wanted to check if the cable was feeding in or out okay. Man, you never grab the cable! Jimmy did and lost the first joints of two fingers. We put them in the refrigerator and sent Jimmy and his joints to the ER. They couldn't put him back together again, but Jimmy ended up suing the company and ended up $7,000 richer for his trouble.

Like I mentioned earlier Jimmy and I were together until the big strike in February of '88. I only saw him once after that at the ferry slip in Manhattan. He worked at several jobs after the strike, from oiler on a motor boat at West Point to a loader on a garbage truck. He finally got a job on the Staten Island Ferry as a deckhand. It was a pretty secure city job. But the first boat that he worked on wasn't a ferry boat; it was a boat that ran from the prison on Riker's Island to Hart's Island, the site of the city's indigent burial ground. Every night unclaimed bodies were transported from Riker's to Hart's for burial by prisoners. Jimmy said that the job was a breeze but the aroma left a lot to be desired. He finally ended up on the Staten Island run, and that's where he is today.

I talk pretty often to Jimmy on the phone, over Christmas '05. He was doing physical rehab,. A couple of months before, he went to the rescue of a woman being attacked by a would-be rapist. He thwarted the attack and the man was arrested, but Jimmy was stabbed several times in the left arm and shoulder. For a while, he lost the use of his arm, but through therapy he made a lot of progress. I told him, "Jimmy, you did good. I'm proud of you. I don't know how I would have reacted. You're my hero!"

# Chapter 11: Winding down

My last year, I really lucked out. The company put the *70* on a jet-fuel run from either Philadelphia or New York to Logan Airport in Boston. It was a sweetheart deal: steady work with a couple of days running between loads. In the winter, when the North Atlantic kicked up, we would go weather-bound until the weather moderated. Once in a while they would throw in a run to Portland up in southern Maine, or a jaunt to Portsmouth, New Hampshire; occasionally I would lighter a load of bonded jet fuel for a foreign airline off of a ship at the anchorage. How I hated the lightering work! The ship would shoot the product to you as fast as you could take it. When you were getting near the end, you'd look up to the deck of the ship, and half the time no one was there. Even if they were, odds were they wouldn't speak English. So now you're frantically looking for someone, *anyone,* to start shutting down before you are up to your knees in oil, and featured on the evening news, picture at 11. Thankfully, I always got away with it, although on a few occasions I did have to call the coast guard. That kind of call always got their full attention.

I was finally down to my last trip: Philadelphia to Boston. The tug with me had Captain Pete Cook in the wheelhouse. He was a good union man and an all-around nice guy; I always enjoyed working with him and his crew on the *Stephen*. On the run down the Delaware River, we passed the *Zachary* heading up. They used to tow me quite a bit. The crew got on the radio and wished me well on my retirement. I was really touched. I liked that whole crew, and they really made me feel good.

It was a nice trip weather-wise, but I had planned on getting off in Boston, and it wasn't going to happen. The weather had kicked up, so the run from the other end of the Cape Cod Canal to Boston would be very sloppy. The tug captain decided to anchor in Buzzards Bay until the weather moderated, That was predicted to be the day after tomorrow. Tomorrow being our normal crew change day, I called my relief, and we agreed to change at the anchorage. He came out on the pilot boat, we went through the crew change routine, and then I loaded my sea bag onto the pilot boat and headed for shore. It was a wet trip in, but I stayed out on deck and watched the *70* grow smaller and smaller. I had tears in my eyes. A way of life that I loved very much had come to an end. I was going to miss it.

The plus side: I would be home for all of the holidays and spend more time with my first love, Judy.

After I retired from the boats in 1999, I didn't stop working completely. I started driving for Magnolia Transportation, a small carrier located in Parsonsburg, Maryland. I pulled a reefer trailer usually up to New England or down to the Carolinas. I did that for five years and decided it was enough; I wanted something a little easier. I took a job at a tool rental shop, checking rented tools in and getting them ready to go out again. Easy enough, except for standing on your feet for ten hours. That was too much for me. My back couldn't take it. I figured that if I wanted to sit on the job I would have to go back to driving. I got a gig with FedEx Ground pulling double trailers from Bridgeville, Delaware, to Harrisburg, Pennsylvania. It's a piece of cake, 320 miles round trip. Takes me about seven hours, and that includes putting the trailers together and breaking them down at each terminal. I also get to use the company cell phone for my own use.

In April off 2001I decided that I had enough  time on my hands to squeeze in another project, I started to build a boat, a twenty-one footer. It had a small cuddy cabin with two vee- bunks and a Porta-Potty, just the right size for Judy and me. I sent away for a set of plans for a twenty-one-foot inboard, but then I came across another boat that I liked better than the first. It was another twenty-one footer, designed by Chesapeake Marine Designs—a very pretty boat. I shelved the first set of plans and decided on the second. The problem was that I didn't know where to begin. I wanted to use bronze screws and bolts to fasten the hull, but nobody seemed to have a clue where I could buy them. Finally Judy made a couple of phone calls to suppliers that her boss used, and she located a company in North Carolina that could supply all of the bronze fasteners that I would need.

Lumber was another problem. All of the so-called big-box stores sold lumber that was suitable for building a house—or so they said; you wouldn't want to build a house with it. It didn't hold fasteners that well and was prone to rot. I wanted to use yellow pine, which they use for boat building in the south, but I had to locate a lumber yard that sold it. I knew it was common in house trusses and pull-down stairways; hence, I called Salisbury Truss. They legally couldn't sell me any, but they did tell me who could: Miles Lumber in Pocomoke City, Maryland, a fifty-mile ride away. However, they had all of the lumber that I would need. So I was off and running. To save money I would buy the lumber as long and wide as I could and then rip it down to the size that I needed. I started using a big brand-name epoxy system, but that proved to be very expensive. I saw an ad in a boat-building magazine for another product that worked out to be much cheaper than the first one, plus it could be used at much lower temperatures. You live and learn.

When the plans arrived in the mail, I couldn't wait to see them. I was disappointed, to say the least: they just looked like a set of drawings of the offsets, showing the dimensions of the frames and floors, with one drawing of the boat in profile. I also got a note from the designer saying that he assumed I had studied and read up on boat building. Luckily I had, but I still faced a challenge.

I started by driving stakes into the ground and building a horizontal ladder frame.on which the actually boat frames would be set up. the frames had to be built plum and square with each other. I determined a base line to measure the height of each frame, erected each frame, trued it up, and braced it to prevent any movement. I used math that I hadn't used since high school! After four years of effort, though, I think it came out pretty good for a first try. I trailered it up to Short's Marine, in Longneck, Delaware, to have a motor installed. It seems that if they don't install it, they don't warranty it. I left it there for three days. My yard seemed empty without the boat, after so long seeing it every time that I looked out of the window. When I brought it back home, there was a problem; the motor could not swing hard left or hard right rudder because the twin skegs on the boat were in the way. They had to go. I lay on my back under the boat with a saw in my hand, staring at the offending skegs. I have to tell you, it takes a lot to make that first cut. Once that saw bites into that wood, you are committed. I had the same feeling when I was staring at the cabin roof before I started cutting for the ventilation hatch. Regardless, I got it done. Now I was concerned that it would affect the handling of the boat, but it had to be done.

I stepped back and looked at my creation. *Okay, what's next?* Then it dawned on me: she was ready to be launched. it was July 10, 2005, I filled the tanks with gas and hooked up the truck to the trailer, and off we went for the boat ramp at Ocean Pines. When we arrived, I backed the trailer down to the water's edge, gave Judy the camcorder to capture the moment, and attached a line to the boat. I didn't want it to sail off without us. The boat was still on the trailer, and the truck was almost awash. I got out, gave the boat a shove, and over she went. She looked great, floating as pretty as you please.

On the ride over to the ramp, we had both been laughing. We felt as if we were on our way to the hospital to deliver a baby. We were both so nervous. Now it just felt good looking at her floating there, me standing in the water up to my knees, and Judy standing on the dock, holding the line that I had given her with a big smile on her face. Then I saw it: the camera lying on the dock. I couldn't believe it. We missed it. It wouldn't be the same if we did it again for the camera. Still, it was a beautiful boat, and I was very proud of the job I did. I couldn't wait until the summer of 2006, hoping that Judy and I could spend more time on the water enjoying the boat. We'd take our dog Katie along with us.

After all of the cutting, bending, and shaping and watching a boat slowly begin to take shape. I took a certain amount of pride in it, building a boat is not the easiest thing in the world. I liked the challenge.

I started on another boat in October 2006. It was a sixteen-foot dory, strictly a rowboat. It would be ideal for someone interested in working out. It would be good exercise. Rowing uses just about every muscle in your arms, back, and legs.

I was building this boat in the garage out of the weather but It was pretty tight quarters. In fact, I was getting plenty of exercise just stepping over everything. I thought it would be a straightforward building job, but it had its frustrating moments. When the weather warmed up it went a little easier. It was a beautiful little boat to row, at the launching I took it for a spin it seemed to just fly across the wave tops.

I think I will take a break on the boat building for awhile. You just can't put these things on a shelf also I'm running out of room. I'll hang a for sale sign on the dory.

# Chapter 12:

My first-driving job was a bit of a fluke. I had just graduated high school. I was seventeen, and no company was going to hire you until you were eighteen, so I was just going through the motions of looking for a job. I was standing on the corner waiting for a bus. I didn't own a car yet it was the same corner that Jimmy Slick and I , waited for the high school bus. We would see these two old men loading barrels of meat into the back of a refrigerated truck that had "Mutual Provisions" painted on the side. Anyway, I'm waiting on the bus and this old man comes up to me and tugs my sleeve. He says, "Sonny, you are maybe looking for a job. I need somebody to drive my truck. I'll pay you sixty-five cents an hour." That was minimum wage at the time. I jumped at it.

The truck was a 1949 Dodge, ton-and-a-half. The guy's name was Sam Troum, he was the owner. The other guy was Ike, the butcher. He was also a survivor of the German concentration camps. He showed me the number that they had tattooed on his arm. When the state lotteries came out a couple of years later, I often wondered if Ike ever played that number. It would have been something if he had won with it and then sent the German government 10 percent for giving him the number.

Ike would go with me on the deliveries, doling out corned beef and brisket and a little pastrami on the side. Before we left in the morning, Ike would stick a big needle gun into the meat and pump it full of brine. The meat would increase in size about four times, and then into the brine it went to keep its size. Loading those brine-filled barrels into the truck was the hardest part of the job. Sammy had quite a business: we delivered that meat all over North Jersey, mostly to diners and restaurants. But all and all, the job sucked. Mr. Troum was a decent guy, and so was Ike, but I came home at night stinking of corned beef. I made all of 26 bucks before taxes—nothing to write home about. I gave Mr. Troum notice on July 25; I was turning eighteen in four days, and then I was starting at Maidenform Brassiere on the first of August alas, I didn't finish the week. My Aunt Rita died the same day I gave notice, and she was buried on my birthday. She was only thirty-six years old and she was my godmother. She lived with us, so I was very close to her, I missed her an awful lot..

August first I started work at Maidenform Brassier Co.starting pay was a buck an hour a couple of weeks later we found out that they were hiring new help and paying them one dollar and two and a half cents per hour we were still making a buck per hour ,we all walked out. They gave us a two and a half cent raise and we went back to work. It didn't matter too much to me. I had already enlisted in Uncle Sam's army; I was leaving the first week in December. Nem, Slick, and Stofif were already away in the Marine Corps.

Donny (Ginky) Langly and I were opting for the army. I would end up in the transportation corps, and he would go into the ordnance corps. We wouldn't see each other again for thirty years, when we all got together at my house in 1985. Where I thoroughly enjoyed my time in the army,

Donny hated it. Different strokes for different folks, I guess. He went on to become a schoolteacher.

Except for working on weekends on Long Island, at Camp St. Regis, I'd never been away from home for any length of time. I now was looking at a minimum of three years. Alas, it all but flew by. I went into the army a kid. In three years, I grew up quite a bit; I was a much wiser twenty-one-year old. I still firmly believe to this day, maybe even more so in today's world, that every high school graduate should serve a mandatory tour in the military, if only to grow up and become a man. Then he can go to college, if he so desires, and I'll bet he takes it a lot more seriously.

When I got out of the army in 1958, I went back to work at Maidenform. They put me in their machinist apprentice program. It was a good trade at the time. It has since been automated to death, and I was almost bored to death. I was learning how to be a tool and die maker—at the time a highly skilled trade—but I was trapped inside this shop all day. And after three years in the army, outdoors almost all of the time, I didn't like it at all. So off I went, over to New York, to Local 333, the tugboat union. I signed up for work as a deckhand or oiler. I had high hopes—which were soon to be dashed. Work was scarce, especially if you didn't know anyone to speak up for you, and I didn't. I got a few jobs working as an oiler in the engine room, for Tracy Towing, mostly on the *Walter Tracy*. But they were few and far between, nothing I could live on. So I got my next driving job.

I started working for Beacon oil co., delivering home heating oil. It was an interesting job, and I got to meet a lot of people. It was also the first of four times that I would work for Beacon. Though they were very good people, they didn't pay that well. We were paid by the gallon to deliver oil, so in the winter you could make pretty decent money, but in the summer the money tree died. Unless you opted to clean furnaces, which paid by the furnace; if you hustled, you could do pretty well. Now I know that sounds like a nasty job, but it wasn't all that bad. You just had to get a system and you would do a good job in about an hour, and five furnaces a day was a good payday. A lot of two-family houses had two furnaces. That was like a bonus. One memorable episode I had was a house in Maplewood, New Jersey. When I arrived, the lady of the house told of noises emanating from the inside of the furnace. With her looking over my shoulder, I opened the furnace door. Lo and behold, a squirrel stared right back at me, and he was pissed. He probably came down the chimney and found himself trapped. He was covered head to toe with soot. I quickly slammed the door; I definitely didn't want him running loose in the house. The customer was alarmed.

"No problem," I assured her. I put my jumper wire across the thermostat connections on the relay and flipped the switch. The furnace lit, and the last look that I got of that squirrel, he resembled a Fourth of July sparkler.

The poor lady, however, was about to pass out. She started yelling, "How could you do such a thing?"

"Easy," I told her. Unless she wanted to reach in there and grab it, I saw no other option. As far as I was concerned, problem solved. Just another day in the life of furnace man. I finished cleaning the furnace—which, by the way, did not yield any remains of said squirrel. I assume that he ended up in my vacuum cleaner.

Delivering heating oil had its moments: overzealous watchdogs looking to take you apart, irate motorists bitching about your double parking, and more. I had one idiot who actually went around the block and backed up against my front bumper to block me. When I was finished I just backed out of the street and left him sitting there. He didn't even have to go around the block to get in front of me; he could have gone around me, like the car before him did. He was just a lousy driver.

Snow definitely made the job more interesting. For one thing, it tended to cover the tank filling pipes, and unless you knew where they were, you were going to do a lot of digging. Luckily I knew. My secret? Magic marker. Draw an arrow on the vent pipe for the tank, and then pace it off. It will usually put you within a couple of inches of the fill. During heavy snow, I even delivered oil with a sled. I would park on the main street, which was usually passable, fill five-gallon cans, and sled them down to customer's tank. That's when even the watchdog was glad to see you.

The winter of 1960 and1961 saw some pretty nasty weather two bad snow storms, leaving about two feet of snow on the ground and nary a snow plow to be had for the side streets. Thankfully there were no fires. I was working for the Railway Express Agency at the time driving a truck in New York. Forget getting to work; no buses were running. Beacon Oil gave me a call and asked if I could help them out making some oil deliveries. Well, being that I couldn't get to New York, I figured why not. Plus, I knew where the tanks were under the snow. I called Jimmy Slick up. He couldn't get to his job either, so he agreed to come along.

We went out with a truckload of oil, and every time I got stuck in the snow, Jimmy pushed me out. He was a big boy. I could only empty the truck halfway, because if I pumped all the oil out, I would be too light and would have no traction on the snow-covered streets. So after I pumped half a load, I would go down to the hook and reload. It was a long day, if I couldn't get the truck through a street to the customer we filled cans and sledded the oil ,Jimmy and I both made a lot of money and kept a lot of people warm.

Railway Express Agency was my next job. It was a nationwide company owned by all of the country's railroads. They picked up rail freight at one end and delivered it at the other. It was a good teamster union job with good pay and benefits. I did pickup and deliveries in New York City and out of the Hoboken terminal. I also drove trailers among the five boroughs and the piggyback yards; for the uninitiated, that was where they put the trailers on flat cars. I did that too, backing trailers down about forty flat cars. You spent your whole night driving backwards. I worked there twice, 1960 to '61, and again from 1963 to '66. The company was losing more and more business. They just couldn't keep up, technology-wise. By 1970 they were gone.

I started by turning out at the terminal on 11th Avenue and Forty-Second Street. I worked nights. There are two kinds of people in New York, night people and day people. The day people are the ones you always see in a hurry, moving shoulder to shoulder, not unlike a school of fish, and always with an attitude. The night people are a little different. The streets and sidewalks are practically deserted, with most of the buildings tucked in for the night, and traffic moves at a more leisurely pace; everybody is a little more relaxed. I would take a truck into the garment center, back into some hole in the wall, and then take a load of clothes back to the terminal. Usually you would take two loads a night, not a bad deal. Later on, I worked a couple of delivery routes, but that was day work and I didn't care for it. I also worked Air Express, which was interesting. Once in a while, I would deliver film to the television studios for the evening news shows. They would be on the air when I went in, Chet Huntley on NBC and Bill Beutel on ABC. I never saw old Walter Cronkite on CBS. If you ever heard them say "Pictures at eleven," I delivered the pictures. Another perk that went with the job was meeting celebrities. I delivered to

Della Reese, the singer, and later the head angel on *Touched by an Angel*—she signed for the package herself. I told her that I liked her singing, which I really did, and she thanked me, and I was on my way. I also met Joan Crawford, the movie actress and, at the time, the owner of Pepsi-Cola. I had to fight with the doorman to make the delivery. He probably thought she'd give out a big tip, which she didn't. All that I got was a big smile and a thank you. But I will say that she looked exactly in person as she does in the movies: nose in the air.

One of the best gigs that I had was the Fulton Fish Market. I worked the market in the fall of '63. I know because that's where I was when Kennedy was shot. My hours were 11:00 A.M. to 8:00 P.M. I would pick up my truck at the terminal at Thirty-Third and Tenth, go down to the Sixteenth Street terminal, and pick up a bag of snails for the market. I would deliver the snails and then pick up all of the fish being shipped out. The places were all closed by that point; they open up at 2:00 A.M. But I had keys for them all. Then I would go to Teddie's House of Sea Food, the only place open, and get my free copy of the *Herald Tribune.* The foreman at Teddie's would let me know if there were any late deliveries. There never were. After that I was off to Carmine's Bar and Restaurant, the big mob hangout. Everybody knew that the mob ran the market. I would have my lunch at about three.. I returned to Thirty-Third Street, unloaded my fish, and went home. At that point it was bout five in the afternoon. At six, I called the dispatcher to ask, "Any late deliveries?"

"No, all clear, kid; bring it in and go home."

"Okay. See you tomorrow."

What a racket! But all good things must come to an end. At Christmas, we got a railway bonus. Happy Layoff. They did it every year. They didn't want to pay us for the two holidays, when it was usually pretty slow. When I came back to work, you know that I didn't get to go back to the market. I ended up with a pickup route—luckily, another breeze. I just parked my truck on East Eighteenth, and they brought the freight to me. The hours were the same except now I had to put in the full eight hours. I would get to my parking spot at about noon, and collect freight until five. Then I would leave, and do four pickups around the block. One of these was Gordon Novelty. They made all of those gag items, like plastic turds and vomit; my favorite was the whoopee cushion. The guy was always giving me the damn things. I used to leave the turd or vomit on the seat of the bus when I got off at my stop. I often wondered how many people would sit down and then quickly jump up and move to another seat, but I was never there to see the fruits of my labors. I'm sure the driver was thrilled when some passenger clued him in.

Railway shipped a lot of weird freight. Dead bodies were a specialty. It was cheaper to ship the dearly departed by rail than by air. It took longer, but it's not like they were in any hurry. I couldn't count the number of caskets that I shuttled between Grand Central Station and Penn Station, or between those stations and the North River Piers, especially American export lines piers. Those ships served the Italian ports. It seems that a goodly number of Italians who died during WWII wanted to be buried in Italy. Twenty years after the war ended, they were digging them up and shipping them out. That was all trailer work. After Judy and I got married in 1964, I bid a trailer job, no freight handling, just drop and hook. In 1966, I left Railway altogether. They were on their way out ,the hand writing was on the wall.

After my short career at tidewater, I then went to work for Metropolitan Petroleum, one of the best jobs I ever had, except for the boats. I worked the winter of '67 and '68. When I got laid off, I immediately went to work for Humble Oil and Refining, now known as Exxon. I Already related what happened there

# Chapter 13:

In 1951 We were living on Humphries Avenue when my mother's sister, my aunt Agnes, and Uncle Andy bought a house up on Avenue E and Forty-Third. We were moving again. My father's friend Whisky, a.k.a. John Gosieski, showed up with his 1932 Cadillac ambulance, which he had cut down to look like a truck. We loaded all of our furniture into it and headed uptown. We looked like a bunch of Okies: my old man sitting up front with Whisky, smoking cigars, and me riding on top of all of the furniture, hoping nobody was around to see me.

We moved everything into the house and settled in. Down on Humphries Avenue, we'd been on the second floor, and my room over the stairs had no heat. I froze my ass off. Lo and behold, this house had the same setup, except this room was smaller! When we put my chest of drawers in the room, I couldn't open the two bottom drawers because they hit the bed. The room also had no window, just a door that opened onto an open porch. At least the door had a windowpane in it. My closet was in the hall—well, if you can call it a closet. It was so shallow that when I put my shirts on hangers, I had to turn the hangers parallel to the closed door. It was good training for my army days, I can say that.

This was a working house, and I felt like Cinderfella. We had a system, a different chore each day of the week. Saturday we scrubbed the floors, and this was no sissy job with a mop. This was with grandma's brown soap, a bucket of water, and a scrub brush. I would start in my mother's kitchen; then it was into the back hall, down the back stairs, and into my aunt's kitchen. I must have done a good job, because I got to do it every week.

My other job was to take care of the heat. What a nightmare! Our heating system consisted of two ancient coal-fired furnaces, one for upstairs and one for downstairs. They squatted right in the middle of the cellar, big and ugly. Each one had this big, long body with all of these long arms coming off the top of it running along the ceiling until they disappeared; it looked like a giant metal octopus. The arms snaked up between the walls to carry the heat—and the soot—through the house. When you woke up in the morning and blew your nose, you would see the soot in your handkerchief, all black, nasty stuff.

Every night I had to go down and bank the furnaces so they'd burn all night. Of course, when you load a furnace up with coal and cut the draft, it doesn't burn that hot, and you freeze your ass off. As soon as I woke up in the morning, I ran downstairs, shook down the furnaces, opened the draft door, and fired those suckers up. Then I emptied out the ashes, and they were good until I came home from school. Since I was already down in the cellar at that point, I also tended the hot water heater, a little pot-bellied affair that burned pea coal.

The heating system chore was a winter job. The furnaces were shut down for the summer, but the hot-water heater ran year-round. It kept the cellar nice and warm in July … just my luck. Still, one advantage to those old coal-fired days was that if you ever found yourself stuck in the snow, you were never too far from someone's ashcan sitting at the curb. All you needed was a little shovel in your trunk.

I left for the army on December 6th, 1955. I came home on leave after basic training in February, and I went into the cellar. There stood this brand-spanking-new oil-fired automatic heating system. Gone were the big ugly octopuses, the coal bins, and last but not least, that little piss-pot hot water heater. I guess nobody wanted the job after I left.

Another improvement my family had made was to my front room bedroom. They took the door out, replaced it with a window, and put in heat. Of course the room was still the size of a closet, but now it was a warm closet. I would no longer wake up with frost on the blanket.

In December of '58, I was released from the army. I came home to my much warmer bedroom, and I met up with the old gang, hanging out at the Venice Tavern down on Cottage Street. Soon it became clear I needed a car. My Uncle Frank's brother-in-law's brother ran a Texaco station up on Fifty-Sixth and Avenue C. He was selling a '51 Dodge. He wanted three hundred bucks for it. I haggled with him for a while, and I got it for three hundred dollars. Apparently I wasn't a very good haggler. I drove it home that day: a big black four-door sedan, twenty-five horsepower under the hood, and a fluid drive transmission. Sweet.

The car ran great until it blew a head gasket, which I replaced, and then it promptly blew that one. I figured that I had a problem, and I was right: turned out the engine had a warped head. I went to Twin City Auto Wreckers and took the head off of a Desoto, which was a Dodge with a different grill. I replaced the warped head with the one from the Desoto. Problem solved! It was a great car after that. I drove it for a year, and then I sold it to my friend Frank Carter so I could buy a brand-new 1960 Chevy four-door.

It would be the last black car that I would buy, though: after being asked to drive for four weddings and two funerals, I put two and two together.

I settled on green for my next car. I was a real traditionalist when it came to cars, I wasn't convinced that power steering and air conditioning were here to stay, so I bought a 1968 Dodge Coronet 440, with a slant six-cylinder engine but neither air nor power steering, My Chevy had given me eight years of yeoman's service, except for the time my sister drove it from Newburgh to Bayonne in low gear at sixty-plus miles per hour (she overheated the engine and burnt out the water pump). When the mechanic told me that the transmission was okay, I was thankful for small favors and figured that I was getting off easy just replacing the water pump. I sold the Chevy to my next-door neighbor's brother. When he came and drove it away, I thought I would cry. I get very attached to things, especially after eight years.

I bought the Dodge because it had a big steering wheel. With the advent of power steering, drivers no longer needed the leverage of a big steering wheel, so manufacturers were changing to these tiny steering wheels I called "pussy wheels." It was like driving those bumper cars from the amusement park! I wanted a man's wheel, so I bought the Dodge. We made a lot of trips to the Jersey Shore with it. The kids were small then; Robbie wasn't even born yet when I bought it. We used to plop them in the back seat—this was before the days of car seats and off we went. I drove and Judy hollered at the kids. Back then a car trip was an enjoyable experience, something to look forward to. Now between the seat belts, the booster seats, and the airbags, a car trip is more like a raid into enemy territory, with an ambush waiting just around the next bend in the road.

A little change of gears here. The year was 1969. We were living at Elsie's house on Twenty-First Street, Elsie was babysitting, and Judy and I were off to the movies in Journal Square. I was driving my 1968 Dodge Coronet 440. That's how I remember the year. The movie was over, and we were on our way home. I exited the parking garage on Pavonia Avenue and was heading down to Westside Avenue. I was driving with one eye on the road and the other eye on my lovely wife, when the eye that was watching the road saw a bright light shining right at it. *Whoa!* It was a beat cop standing in the middle of the street, shining his flashlight at me. For all of you young people, a beat cop actually walked his beat, as opposed to riding around in a patrol car. It made for a much safer neighborhood. Anyway, he was in front of my car. I either stopped or I hit him. He ran around to the passenger side and got in. "Follow that car." He pointed to a set of fast-disappearing taillights. Thankfully, I have this powerful slant-six engine under the hood. I'm up to the task. This guy in front of me was going to look in his rearview mirror and all he'd see was Dodge. While we were in pursuit down Westside Avenue blowing all of these traffic lights (for some reason they were all red when I got to them), the cop told me what his beef was. It seems this guy went through a stop sign, and when my boy here flagged him down, he tried to run over him. I agreed with him. I'd be pissed off too.

I felt sorry for Judy. This guy was pretty big to begin with, plus he had this big overcoat on. With all of the junk that cops wear or carry around—gun, nightstick, handcuffs, etc.—she was crushed between us. All of a sudden, he turned into Lincoln Park. I followed him into the park, but we lost him. The cop asked me to drive him back to his beat. "Sure, no problem." I ran him back to Sip Avenue. End of story. Not quite. After we dropped him off, we turned back toward Bayonne. We were talking about the excitement after the movie, and I thought we were going to end up on candid camera. We stopped for the light at Union Street and Westside Avenue. All of a sudden we were surrounded by Jersey City's finest. "Out of the car!" I got out of the car. They start rattling off all of these crimes: speeding down Westside Avenue, going through five red lights, etc. "Who the hell do you think you are?" I interjected a powerful "but" between each accusation, but they weren't listening. Their adrenaline was flowing, and the quarry was right in front of them. I was about to make their night. Then I told them I thought I was the concerned citizen who, in complete disregard for my own safety, went out of my way to assist an officer in need of help. Finally the lights went on. "Was that you?" "Yep, that was me." After that they would have kissed my ass in Macy's window. They couldn't do enough for us. We just want to get the hell out of there! After that they gave each cop his own car to chase the bad guys.

After all of the excitement of my very brief career in law enforcement, Judy and I were glad to get the hell out of Jersey City and back to Bayonne. I don't think Judy and I ever took in another movie there.

# CHAPTER 14:

... 1978 we moved from Bayonne to Point Pleasant. That brought mixed feelings for me: I loved Bayonne, but it had changed a lot. Houses were out of sight, price-wise. We had gone in on a house with Judy's parents, but after a while Judy and I both realized that we wanted our own house, and to do that we had to look out of town. At the time I was driving a truck for Metropolitan Petroleum, in Jersey City, so we didn't want to move too far away. We eventually settled on Point Pleasant, sixty miles away but affordable.

We moved into our new home at 800 Barton Avenue in February, a Friday. The next Monday, I left for work up in Jersey City at 4:00 a.m. It was snowing when I left. It snowed all the way up, all of that day, and night. In fact, it snowed about twenty-seven inches. I didn't get home until Thursday, and Judy had the driveway all shoveled for me. I pulled the Dodge in, glad to finally be home. Then I went to open the car door ... no dice. My wife should have been a gravedigger! She dug out just enough for the car to get in, but forgot that you had to open the door to get out of the car.

We liked Point Pleasant. It wasn't crowded as we were used to in Bayonne, but that was not to last. It seems that word got out about our move, and everybody started to follow us down. In no time it was just like Bayonne.

After a few years we sold Barton Avenue and moved to 1816 Bay Boulevard. We bought a much bigger house, in Bay Head Shores, a small beach community within Point Pleasant. Even though we paid a lot for the house, we sold it for double the price two years later. Judy, the real estate whiz. We then moved to Oriole Way, on the other side of town. By now our dog Trixie had had it up to here with moving. We had to take her to the vet and get her tranquilized. In December, when I took the Christmas decorations down from the attic to trim the tree, she took one look at the boxes and thought we were moving again. I had to make another trip to the vet.

Well you guessed it A little while later, Trixie was right: we were moving again, on our way to Maryland. We listed the house on Oriole Way, only this time Judy's magic didn't work. It took a while to sell and we didn't make the money that we thought we would. In the meantime, we rented a town house in Barnegat, New Jersey. The plan was to rent the house until we were ready to make the leap south to Maryland, and let Robbie and Nancy take over the place. It was not to be.

I was working on the barge *Richmond*, so I was away at the time. On the Friday before Memorial Day weekend, the town shut our water off. They claimed that the owners of the property did not have a certificate of occupancy, and therefore we could not legally live in the house. I guess they were in the right, but why did they wait until Nancy was in the in the shower, all soaped up, to shut it off?

The landlord ran a hose from his house to give us water. The town quickly cut it off. Judy went to see the mayor, who gave her the old "My hands are tied" routine, but he did get the water turned on for the weekend. I came home on Tuesday, and we started  frantically looking for an apartment—but where do you find an apartment for four adults on a day's notice? Impossible! Enter my friend and co-worker Ed Parker, a tug captain for Morania. He had recently gotten a divorce and kept the house, which sat empty while he was away. I called Morania's port captain and explained the situation, and he in turn got in touch with Eddy, who gave us the name of the neighbor holding the key to his house, and . We moved right in.

We rented an apartment for Robbie and Nancy in Pt. Pleasant. Now we figured all we had to do was wait out the summer in Eddy's house, then load up all of our junk and head for Ocean City … and get a winter rental while we built our house..

In the meantime a reporter for the Asbury Park Press, our local paper, gets in touch with us. Seems he wanted to write an article about us, painting us as this poor family that got run over rough-shod by the town of Barnegat, literally thrown out into the street not through any fault of their own, but because they were caught in the middle of an ongoing battle between the landlord and the town. The town claimed that the landlord was not licensed to rent, but somehow they never stopped him from advertising or maintaining a rental office. The reporter wrote a full-page article describing our trials and tribulations and pretty much criticized the way the town handled the whole thing. We had our fifteen minutes of fame, although all we got out of it was an all-expense paid trip for our furniture to the storage facility.

Meanwhile back at the ranch, Eddy had come home; Judy and I heard him moving around the house half of the night. In the morning Judy got up to go to work and then came back to the bedroom to inform me that we had no water. What the hell is this, Barnegat's revenge? Not again!

I got up and found Eddy beside himself with worry. Water was bubbling out of the ground on his front lawn; we had no way to shut it off without calling the water department. "So what's the problem? Call 'em," I shrugged.

Eddy looked embarrassed, and then told me about his in-ground sprinkler system. It seems that he teed into the water line before it got to the meter. I realized immediately what he meant; he'd been getting a free ride every time he watered the lawn, and now he was looking at payback. He kept pacing back and forth across the kitchen floor, carrying on about how they were going to put him in jail and throw the key away. Talk about drama: he had his wrists extended as if to say, "Put the cuffs on me and take me away. If only I could undo what I have done. I'll never cheat again!"

We Eventually called the water department. We had no choice; we had to shut the water off before we could do anything. A guy came over in a pickup truck, looked at the geyser in the front lawn, and proceeded to shut the water off. He never said a word about the flood, just told us to call when we wanted it turned back on, and left.

Judy left for work, and Eddy and I started our excavation of the front lawn. When Judy came home, all she saw was this huge pile of dirt and our shovels throwing more out of the hole. Needless to say we found the leak, right at that sneaky tee, repaired it, and then moved it to the legal side of the meter. Eddy told us how he had found the leak during the night, and imagined all of these worst-case scenarios. He swore he learned his lesson. We called and the water man came back, turned the water back on, and left. Eddy breathed a sigh of relief and went to bed.

September was upon us before we realized it, and it was to time to hit the road. We loaded all of our stuff, and off we went to new horizons. Maryland here we come.

# CHAPTER 15: BACK TO BAYONNE

When I was growing up in Bayonne, during and right after World War II, things were a lot different from the way they are today. Nobody lived out of town: my mother had seven brothers and sisters, and they and their families all lived in Bayonne. My father also had seven brothers and sisters, and except for Aunt Mary they also all lived in Bayonne. The holidays were always mob scenes, but I loved it. Christmas meant all of the Vargovciks gathering at Grandma Vargovcik's house. On Christmas Eve, we would enjoy mushroom soup, *halushki, babalkis,* and all of the homemade Slovak cakes—after, of course, we all partook of the Christmas wafers, or *oplatki.* Oplatki were similar to the Holy Communion wafer. We'd put a little honey on it and down it went! We each had a white wafer, and my grandfather, as the head of the family, had a pink one. After dinner, we would exchange presents, Uncle Ziggy playing Santa Claus.

One thing we never did was go to Midnight Mass. Mushroom soup was made with sauerkraut juice, and a nice hot bowl of soup was the equivalent of about three boxes of Ex-Lax. If you ate that before going to church, well, you might make it through Mass ... barely. At least no one lived more than ten minutes away.

On Christmas morning, we got up at seven to go to 8:00 a.m. Mass. We knew Santa had been there; we could peek through the sliding doors that separated the living room and dining room. Those doors would remain closed until we came home from church. By then my Aunt Agnes and Uncle Andy, and Edna and Bill Cane, my mother's cousins, would be there. They didn't have any kids, so my sister and I were their Christmas joy. Then, later on, my Uncle Vince and Grandpa Lee would stop in for a Christmas drink, a couple of shots and beers. They were all there the year I got the big lump of coal in my stocking. I thought I would never live that down.

One year Uncle Vince came in with this tremendous box, saying it must have been left at his house by mistake. I swear it was as big as a refrigerator. Man, I was all excited, and greedy as you can get. I started tearing at the wrapping paper. I ripped open the box, and there was another box inside. I ripped open that box and there was another box inside of that one! This went on and on until I was down to a box the size of a shoe box. I ripped at that box—it had to be the last one. It was. Inside was something wrapped up in paper. I tore at the paper to reveal … another lump of coal. Everybody was hysterical by then. Me, I just figured that I'd pissed somebody off big time.

After that fiasco, we all went over to Grandma Lee's house for our traditional boiled chicken dinner. The adults told and retold the story of me and the boxes, much to everybody's delight. It was threatening to turn in to one of those Christmas tales that grows every year.

Luckily for me the war was over, and all of the men were coming home. I now had cousins coming out of the woodwork. Christmas was changing. The family was getting so big that we couldn't fit in one house. Then Aunt Josie and Uncle Phil moved to Clark Township, and Aunt

Annie and Uncle Frank moved to Jersey City. That meant we had a couple of Christmas dinners going on instead of the whole family being together. I never realized it when I was younger, but we never had a dinner at Uncle Richie's house or at Uncle Vince's; it was always at Aunt Annie's, Aunt Josie's, Aunt Agnes's, or my mother's. When it came to food, the house belonged to the woman, it seemed. Thank heavens we didn't have to go to Grandma Lee's anymore for that boiled chicken.

Of course we still went there for the regular Sunday dinner, but the plus side of that was that after dinner the men usually went en masse to Bob Vandabec's saloon, and I got to tag along. I loved hanging out with all of my father's cronies; they were always a lot of fun, always good for a couple of sodas and a couple of games of shuffleboard. Then I got to ride home with my old man half-lit, which meant watching a pro in action. He could drive the Oldsmobile as well loaded as he did sober. We would drop my mother and sister off at the house, and then we 'd drive around to Twenty-Eighth Street and put the car in the garage. I'd jump out and swing open the doors (overhead doors hadn't been invented yet), and the old man would ease that Olds in there, one inch clearance on the right side so the driver would be able to open the door and get out of the car. When I closed the garage doors, they would just kiss the rear bumper: perfect! Then we would walk home. I used to enjoy those walks. My father and I never spent very much time together just the two of us, so when we did, I really enjoyed it.

My father was a sailor. He spent his whole working life on the water, from tug boats to deck lighters. He did it for over forty years. I always wanted to follow in his footsteps, and I did. Those Sundays we spent riding around the harbor shaped my future.

My father was pretty sharp. He didn't have very much schooling, but he was a smart man. He was also very stubborn, and short on patience with a lot of people. For him, you either were or you weren't.

He was very good with his hands; he built some very nice benches and lawn furniture when we had the house at Union Beach. And he did it all with old-fashioned tools, no power tools. I'm still using some of his tools today, although Judy spoils me with power tools. You still have to fall back to the old hand tools on occasion.

One incident I remember very well. It concerned the Oldsmobile. Its original color was battleship gray, which after about ten years was pretty dull and flat. "Come on," my dad said to me. "Let's paint the car." We drove down to the hardware store, where he bought a can of black stove paint. Before the fancy gas and electric ranges that we have today, people had coal or kerosene stoves in their kitchens. At the end of each winter, the stoves looked pretty ratty: all the heat that that they were putting out during the winter pretty much burnt all of the paint off. So in the spring most everyone would go out and buy stove paint to spruce up their kitchen stove. My father bought a can to spruce up the Olds. We each took a brush and started painting. I couldn't believe the finished product; the car looked great. It shone like a new dime. When He junked it a few years later it still looked good.

I got my first car when I was seventeen years old, finally old enough for my license. On July 29 I ventured on down to the DMV and got my permit. I now had to wait ten days before I could take my road test. That was when we were supposed to be taking driving lessons. But the truth be known, hell, we were all aces by then. In fact, working out on Long Island that spring, I wrecked a car. I was with a girl named Penny. We were in her mother's car, driving down some pitch-black country road. I missed a turn and drove into the woods. Lucky for me the sheriff thought I was in the army stationed at a local anti-aircraft battery. He put in his report that I blew a front tire and ran off the road, but actually it was the other way around. Anyway, my biggest problem was getting someone with a car that I could use for the test. Along came Bill Brunnel. I knew him from our days at St. Joseph's. He was tooling around in his father's brand-new 1954 Ford. He drove me up to Roosevelt Stadium in Jersey City. Needless to say, I aced the test. Now that I had a license, I needed wheels. Enter Uncle Ziggy, my father's brother-in-law. He lived out in Piscataway, NJ. And he had a 1938 Chevy sitting next to his barn for a couple of years. I offered him fifteen bucks for it. When I gave him that fifteen bucks, I was broke. That was my whole stash. I couldn't afford plates, so a friend of mine towed me back to Bayonne. Eventually, I got it registered and insured. The car looked like hell. It was covered with rust—not the eating out-the-body rust, more like the sitting-out-next-to-the-barn rust. The upholstery was shot, but the damn thing ran like a clock. It was a great-running car, but not a car you would want to drive your date in. I ended up selling it for ten bucks. That was it for me owning a car on my own for a while. But I did chip in on a couple of wrecks that were hiding behind the used car lot's office. They were in the ten- or twenty-dollar range. I remember in particular a 1935 Plymouth that we had to replace the tar paper roof because it leaked so badly. It was like riding around in a convertible. That was the same car that we blew a brake hose on and lost all of the fluid. We pinched off the blown line, filled the master cylinder with evaporated milk, and drove around with three wheel brakes. There was John Stoffic's Olds with the loose rear axle. It defied all of our efforts to fix it. I think John ended up using it for target practice.

Then there were the high-end cars. Bill Muller had a 1949 Mercury that we cruised around in. Joe Pularki had a beautiful 1941 Pontiac. It was his pride and joy. Nobody piled into that car. There was definitely no shortage of cars. We chipped in for gas, and off we went. Bill Nemik and I were in the same boat as far as owning a car. We were both working at the Foodserver Market, and the Broadway bus looked pretty good to us.

# CHAPTER 16:

Smoking! Pretty cool at one time, everybody did it. I started in 1952, at fifteen years old, and I have my good friend Bill Nemik to thank—well, him and his mother's Viceroy filtered cigarettes. He swiped half a dozen from her pack, and we were off and running, or walking anyway, down Broadway, just puffing away. We were really into it. I held the butt between my fingers, but Nemik let it just hang out of the corner of his mouth, one eye closed to keep it from tearing from the smoke, both hands in his pockets. I'm sure he must have seen that in a movie somewhere, and I would have bet it was a Robert Mitchum flick. We each inhaled three butts without so much as a little cough, and we were hooked.

We each got an allowance of about three bucks a week, Even though both of us were working, we forked our pay to our parents, and in return we got about three dollars each week as allowance. They figured if we had no money to spend, we would stay out of trouble. They were right; even back then you didn't get much mileage out of three bucks. We started buying loosies, four for a nickel, and boy were they terrible. You inhaled them, and you thought you were gagging, but you toughed it out despite your eyes tearing and your throat being on fire. Eventually you got used to it, but Nemik and I figured the wings had to go. My father smoked Chesterfields, so I chose those. I figured in a pinch I could swipe some of his.

The problem with smoking without parental approval was nicotine-stained fingers. I couldn't walk around forever with my hands in my pockets. Bill to the rescue. "You just rub lemon juice on your fingers and presto, nicotine stain is gone," he told me. He was right. Chemistry class had some benefits after all.

Well as slick as I thought I was, I got caught. I might have gotten the nicotine stains off of my fingers, but it's not that easy to get stink of cigarette smoke out of your clothes. My mother told me one day that if I was going to smoke, I could smoke in the house. I was shocked! That was big time; nobody that I knew had permission to light up in their house. Even so, I never did. I couldn't bring myself to smoke in front of my parents. Three years later I was in the army stationed at Fort Dix and my mother and father came to visit me. Having been away from home for a while I wasn't thinking and I lit up in front of them. My mother commented that it was the first time she had seen me smoking.

In the army I switched to Camels because while stationed in the Arctic they ran out of Chesterfields. I figured it was okay; after all, John Wayne and Tyrone Power were always telling us how great Camels were I smoked Camels until I quit in 1968, on the day Nixon was elected. By then they had decided that smoking was going to kill you, so I figured it was time to quit. Another reason to quit was the price of cigarettes. When I smoked they cost around thirty cents a pack. Now they are up around 6 or 7 bucks a pack. You're talking serious money here: a pack a day for a month, and you're out a big chunk of a mortgage payment.

Smoking soon lost its glamour and became just another nasty habit. Up in the Arctic, we hauled a lot of fuel ashore in our boats. It was all in fifty-five gallon drums: gas and diesel fuel. We were surrounded by gasoline vapors, making smoking out of the question. Instead, we chewed. I preferred plug tobacco. You cut it with a knife, stuck it in the corner of your mouth, and let it just sit there while you sucked the juice out and spat it on the deck. Our Eskimo workers were partial to cut tobacco, and they were always offering it to us. You could only refuse so many times without being branded as insufferably rude, so once in a while we took a piece, palmed it, and later threw it over the side. Eskimos left a lot to be desired in the personal hygiene department.

In 1951 we moved to my Aunt Agnes and Uncle Andy's house on Avenue E and Forty-Third Street. The rest of the family was bailing out and leaving town; Aunt Annie and Uncle Frank moved to Brown Place in Jersey City, a street so narrow you needed a shoe horn to get a car down it, and forget finding a parking place. Then Aunt Josie and Uncle Phil moved out to Clark Township, real farm country back in those days. I remember going there for Thanksgiving dinner. The whole family was there, so it was wall-to-wall people. If you happened to be sitting back against the wall and had to go to the bathroom, lots of luck; you should have thought of that before you sat down. I delivered heating oil to Aunt Jo, and before I left to go out there, I would stop at Reith's Bakery and pick up these cookies that she liked. It seems that you could only get them at Reith's.

Uncle Vince and Aunt Helen moved to Howell Township, chicken farm country. Once Uncle Vince got his driver's license, there was no holding him back. Even Uncle Richie and Aunt Irene moved. They left that three-room apartment on Twenty-Ninth Street that they lived in for about fifty years and moved into a three-room apartment on Humphries Avenue. Theresa and Joe lived downstairs, and they lived upstairs.

Not to be left behind, the Vargovciks started bailing out. Aunt Mary and Uncle Ziggy had lived out in Dunnellen, New Jersey, as long as I can remember, so I guess they shouldn't be included in the exodus. But my father's brother Steve took a job up in Buffalo, so he and Aunt Stella and my cousins Billy, Tiny, and Raymond, all shuffled off to Buffalo. Billy got an appointment to West Point and served over twenty years in the army, retiring as a bird colonel. Tiny and her husband, Mike, whom she met in Buffalo, moved out to California, where they ended up in the industrial battery business. After college, Raymond went to work for Ford up in Michigan. Uncle Steve and Aunt Stella eventually moved west to California, near Tiny. Uncle Steve died out there. They shipped his body back to Bayonne, and the whole family gathered for the funeral. We were sad about Uncle Steve dying, but we were glad to see the cousins again. A week later, Aunt Stella and Tiny went back to California, Raymond went home to Michigan, and Billy went back to the army. A week later, Aunt Stella up and died. She was shipped back to Bayonne, and again the whole family gathered for the funeral. We saw Uncle Steve's family more in those two weeks than we saw them in twenty years.

Not to be outdone, Uncle Micky and Aunt Ronnie moved to a new house in Cranford, New Jersey, a nice little ranch that Uncle Micky never stopped working on. I guess it was therapy for him. We used to visit them often. Judy's sister, Carol, lived down the street from them. On one visit, after I had started working on the boats and had grown a beard, we rang the doorbell, and instead of the usual happy greeting, Uncle Micky threatened to throw me out. Of course I wasn't in yet, but I guess that didn't matter. In his generation, only bums and hippies grew beards. Aunt Ronnie quickly interceded and calmed him down, but I detected a few grumbles now and then. After we left, he must have heard about it from Aunt Ronnie, because on subsequent visits I had my beard, but he had no comment.

Uncle Micky always had some advice for me. One thing he repeated a lot was that I should always have a good friend aboard."Gotta have someone there," he'd say. "On a barge, there are only two of you. The other guy better be a friend, or you're both in trouble." I agreed, although if I didn't get along with my mate, it wasn't too difficult to have him taken off; the company didn't want any trouble aboard the boats. Uncle Micky also gave me a set of foul weather gear, and a coat that had belonged to Aunt Ronnie's brother, who was an officer in the army during WWII. It was one of his field coats. The rain gear I didn't need, since I wore only Helle Hansen, the best money could buy. We used to knock the Norwegians about a lot of things, but they did make the best foul-weather gear and sea boots. The army coat was a three-quarter length affair with a wool lining. It weighed a ton when it was dry, and when it was wet, forget about it. Still, it was the warmest coat I ever owned. I could stand a six-hour watch in January in Portland, Maine, the temperature hanging at around zero degrees, a good wind blowing, and I would be reasonably warm even if my beard turned to a chunk of ice. I wore that coat until it literally fell apart.

Aunt Ronnie passed away, and Uncle Micky was devastated. After all those years of it being just him and her, he didn't know how to be alone. I didn't go to her funeral because I was away on the boat. I was also away when Uncle Micky died, and Uncle Andy and Aunt Agnes, too. Some very wise old man once said you should go to all of your friends' and relatives' funerals, or they won't come to yours. At least I had a good excuse.

# CHAPTER 17: IN APRIL

I retired from the boats in 1999, and right away I missed the boat life. I think I have adjusted pretty well. I like spending more time with Judy, and I still got to travel. When I was driving over the road with Magnolia Transportation Judy went on a couple of trips with me and I enjoyed having her come along. In 2004 I left Magnolia and went to work for Fedex Ground, I was looking for shorter trips. I pulled double trailers from Seaford De. to Harrisburg Pa.it was about a six or seven hour day I did it twice a week. After three years I decided to pack it in, no more driving for me, too much aggravation. I need a nice cushy job where I can sit on my ass, maybe on a bar stool.

The other night Judy and I went out to a restaurant called the Blue Ox and did just that. It's a pretty fancy steak house, and pricey to boot but Paulo, my son-in-law, came through with a gift certificate so we figured "What the hell, let's see how the other half lives." It wasn't all that bad. We went for happy hour, sat at the bar, and ordered off of the light fare menu. The shrimp were excellent, but Judy said the French fries were not cutting it. But anyway, where am I going with this? Sports.

I'm not a big sports fan—not anymore, anyway—but I used to be. I was a fanatical fan of the Brooklyn Dodgers. I lived and breathed the Dodgers. When I was a kid, we had no TV. We were glued to the radio for every game, and they were played mostly in the afternoon, so young kids could hear all of the action. When there was no game on, which was usually when they were on the road, we played poker for baseball picture cards. The ante was three in the pot and two for high spade. I had all of the Dodgers in my collection. The other teams, including the despised Yankees, were used to support my gambling habit. When the Dodgers were uprooted and shipped off to Los Angeles, I was devastated. They had finally beat the Yankees in the World Series, and then they were gone. I was in the army at the time, stationed in Fort Story, VA. And my whole outfit were all southerners, and I have to say, they didn't really care a whole lot about the Dodgers moving to LA. So I was kind of alone in my misery. I was never much of a sports fan after that. I tried again when the Mets arrived in New York, but it was never the same.

When we arrived at the Blue Ox, there were only two seats open, and they weren't next to each other. There was a gentleman sitting in between them. He was very gracious and moved over. We started talking sports. When I was decking on the tug *Emily Jean*, my watch partner was a fellow by the name of Cecil Rhodes. Who the hell is Cecil Rhodes? Well, he was a pretty good major league ballplayer. He played for the New York Giants and made the move with them to San Francisco. He was the hero of, I believe, the 1954 World Series. He played under the name of Dusty Rhodes. He had legally changed his name from Cecil to Dusty. I told him that I didn't blame him. Cecil, whew! Dick Young, a very good sports writer for the once-great *Daily News*, noted that you didn't want to be smoking when you interviewed Dusty Rhodes. He liked his booze, and his breath was considered flammable.

Dusty was a great storyteller. We would sit around the galley table while Dusty regaled us with stories of his glory days in the major leagues. He went to most of the old-timers' day games, and after the game they'd go out and party hearty. He was definitely a party person. He would do the rubber chicken circuit, as he called it. All winter they had these sport dinners for fathers and sons, business leaders, etc. He'd give a little talk and crack a few jokes. Years later he was still in demand.

The last time I saw Dusty was at the union meeting just before the strike/lockout of 1988. He and Ginger—the woman who owned the bar outside of the Moran Towing maintenance yard in Port Richmond, Staten Island—were getting married and moving to Florida. He was done with tugboating. I'd bet he's still doing the rubber chicken circuit.

On May 23, 2008, I was at it again. I launched a new career as an Ocean City bus driver. I never drove a bus before, but I had the endorsement on my CDL. I figured what the hell. I always said if it had wheels, I could drive it. In fact, driving a bus is just driving a bigger car. The day after I submitted my application, I got a phone call from the operations manager. I had the job, just like that. We went to two days of indoctrination. There were sixty-two of us. I went out with an experienced driver for two days to learn the fare system. There are about twelve different fares in use. After that I just waited for my start day on May 23. I was working 11:30 AM to 8 PM. And I had the same days off as Judy—Wednesday, Saturday, and Sunday.

I had heard a lot of horror stories about driving the OC buses. There were the kids raising hell, and buses packed to the bursting point and drunks throwing up (Thank god I never had that problem. I had to put up with the rest of it.

Ocean City starts their summer off with the June bugs. These are the recently graduated seventeen- and eighteen-year-old high school students. Mommy and Daddy give them a pocketful of money and send them to OC for a week of hell-raising. To keep them out of big-time trouble, Ocean City lets them ride the bus for free. All they have to do is sit through a one-hour class on the evils of alcohol. Then they get a brightly colored bracelet to wear, and the bus is their limo for the week. And they use it. I would pick them up from the beach soaking wet, leaving puddles of water behind. I started letting people come on with food and drinks that didn't last long. A couple of Happy Meals and supersize Cokes on the deck put an end to that. The worst spill I had was from the old man coming from an Italian restaurant with his doggie bag, a big Styrofoam tray that I knew was filled with pasta and sauce, lots of sauce. He needed two hands to pull himself up the step of the bus, and one of those hands held the tray of pasta, which went from horizontal to vertical and emptied the pasta all over the steps. What a mess. I cleaned it up as best I could, but I had to scrub down the bus when I ended the run. As much as I would have liked to, you can't ban doggie bags.

On one occasion, I had a young girl get on carrying an ice cream cone with a big scoop of soft ice cream. I pointed to the sign reading "No food or drink allowed." I told her that she could enjoy her cone sitting on the bus stop bench and catch the next bus. What did she do? She put the cone in her pocketbook and sat down. I watched in my interior mirror, sure that I would catch her sneaking a taste of her ice cream, but she rode to the end of the line, got off my bus, and boarded the park-and-ride shuttle bus, still carrying the ice cream in her purse. I could feel the "up yours" vibes flowing from her to me, but it was her pocketbook, not mine.

Two bucks and you ride all day—that's a real bargain. Passengers paid the two bucks and I gave them a daily pass.

The pass changed daily. Sometimes it was the letter of the alphabet or a color. People would board and show last week's or yesterday's pass. When I pointed out the obvious, they would swear that the morning driver gave them the pass. The lengths some people will go to for a free ride! Sneaking in the back door was a favorite, but they didn't know that we had a system of mirrors in the bus that even with people standing in the aisles we could see the stairwell of the rear door and anybody hiding there.

I loved dealing with the passengers. They were on vacation and just looking to have a good time. They would get on and tell me where they wanted to go, and my memory surprised me: "Next stop, Mackey's Fish Tales." The most popular destination was Seacrets. Personally I stayed away from the place. When you have more security people than patrons, my antenna goes up. At closing time, the Ocean City Police Department would order as many empty buses as they thought necessary. As the revelers came out, they were given the choice of the bus or the Breathalyzer. Most of them picked up their cars in the morning.

As a bus driver in Ocean City, you run the gamut of passengers—from little old ladies to snotty kids to surly drunks—and I had them all at one time or another.

All of the OC buses were handicap friendly. We had wheelchair lifts, which we used quite often. It was a bit of an inconvenience for the other passengers. Seats had to be folded up to make room for the chair, and people lost their seats, plus it took extra time to lift the chair up onto the bus. If it was raining, it involved me getting a wet ass. On one particular day, I was told by dispatch to leapfrog two crowded buses to pick up a passenger in a wheelchair. I got to the bus stop, and the wheelchair was waiting. It was one of those little scooters that they advertise on TV. I set the bus up to load the chair and drop the lift. My handicapped fare got up out of his chair, got on the bus through the front door, and took a seat, while I loaded his chair and tied it down. This guy looked as healthy as anybody on that bus, but who knows. I got paid by the hour, so why complain. But I couldn't help thinking about the son or daughter getting a handicap plate for Dad, and five years after he died, they still get it renewed so that they can get that prime parking space. He must have thought the handicapped rode free, because when I asked for the two-dollar fare, he was taken back, but he coughed it up. I had wheelchair people so heavy that they made the bus lean when I started lifting them.

Speaking of heavy lifting, every year OC hosted the Maryland State firefighters' convention. They got a free pass to ride the bus, and ride it they did, except for the parade. Then they rode the fire engine When overweight people boarded the bus, they grabbed the handrails, pulled themselves up the step, and practically dumped me out of my seat. I thought to myself, *How in the hell do these people climb ladders and fight fires?* As big as some of them were, they could probably huff and puff and blow the damn thing out.

I finished up on the buses in 2009. I was unemployed, something that I've never been in my whole life. I figured that I'd get another job, but alas, it was not to be. I submitted applications all over, but to no avail. Now it is November 2010, and here I sit in front of this word processor, and things are looking up. Judy and I bought a 14-by-24-foot workshop and set it up in the backyard. I have lots of projects to keep me busy around the house, plus a couple of boats I'd like to build. After that, who knows.

The winters seem to be getting colder and longer. Judy and I may just head south. We're both ready for a new adventure. As long as there are the Knights of Columbus and an Elks lodge, we'll meet new friends, no problem. I'll let you know how we make out.

All done for now

# About the Book

This is a story about a young kid growing up in the blue-collar town of Bayonne, NJ. During the war years of the 1940s and his teenage years of the 1950s, Robert Vargovcik went off to make his mark on the world. Bayonne is located across the harbor from the southern tip of Manhattan. It was known for its oil refineries, but it also had a lot of heavy industries, chemical plants, foundries, and the like. Everybody had a good-paying job. The author grew up in close neighborhoods, and television and air-conditioning were on the distant horizon. It was the time of screen doors, front porches, and backyard swings. Evenings were spent with neighbors exchanging gossip and waiting for a cool breeze. Winters were spent playing board games. Thanks to gas rationing, the streets were the playgrounds, and seven-year-olds could roam far and wide and not worry their parents. They just had to make sure they were home for dinner.